THE MARVELS OF ROME

MIRABILIA URBIS ROMAE

Other Historical Travel Guides
Published by Italica Press

The Marvels of Rome for the Macintosh and Windows

Theoderich, *Guide to the Holy Land*

Pierre Gilles, *The Antiquities of Constantinople*

William Fitz Stephen, *Norman London*

Enrico Bacco, *Naples: An Early Guide*

The Pilgrim's Guide to Santiago de Compostela
(Codex Calixtinus) by William Melczer

The Road to Compostela for the Macintosh and Windows

Damião de Góis, *Lisbon in the Renaissance*

THE MARVELS OF ROME

MIRABILIA URBIS ROMAE

Francis Morgan Nichols
Editor and Translator

Second Edition
With New Introduction,
Gazetteer and Bibliography
by
Eileen Gardiner

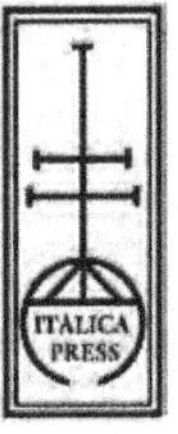

ITALICA PRESS
NEW YORK
1986

First Published 1889,
Ellis and Elvey, London
and
Spithover, Rome

*

Second Edition

ITALICA PRESS, INC
595 Main Street
New York, New York 10044

Library of Congress Cataloging-in-Publication Data
Mirabilia Romae. English.
The Marvels of Rome = Mirabilia Urbis Romae.
Translation of: Mirabilia Romae.
Bibliography: p.
Includes index.
1. Rome (Italy)—Description—476-1420—Guide-books. 2. Pilgrims and pilgrimages—Italy—Rome. 3. Monuments—Italy—Rome. 4. Legends—Italy—Rome.
I. Nichols, Francis Morgan, 1826- . II. Gardiner, Eileen. III. Title. IV. Title: Mirabilia Urbis Romae.
DG805.M57 1986 914.5'632044 86-45750
ISBN 978-0-934977-02-9 (pbk.)

Printed in the United States of America
9 8 7 6

Cover Illustration: James Stokoe, Cover Design: Caroline Lee.

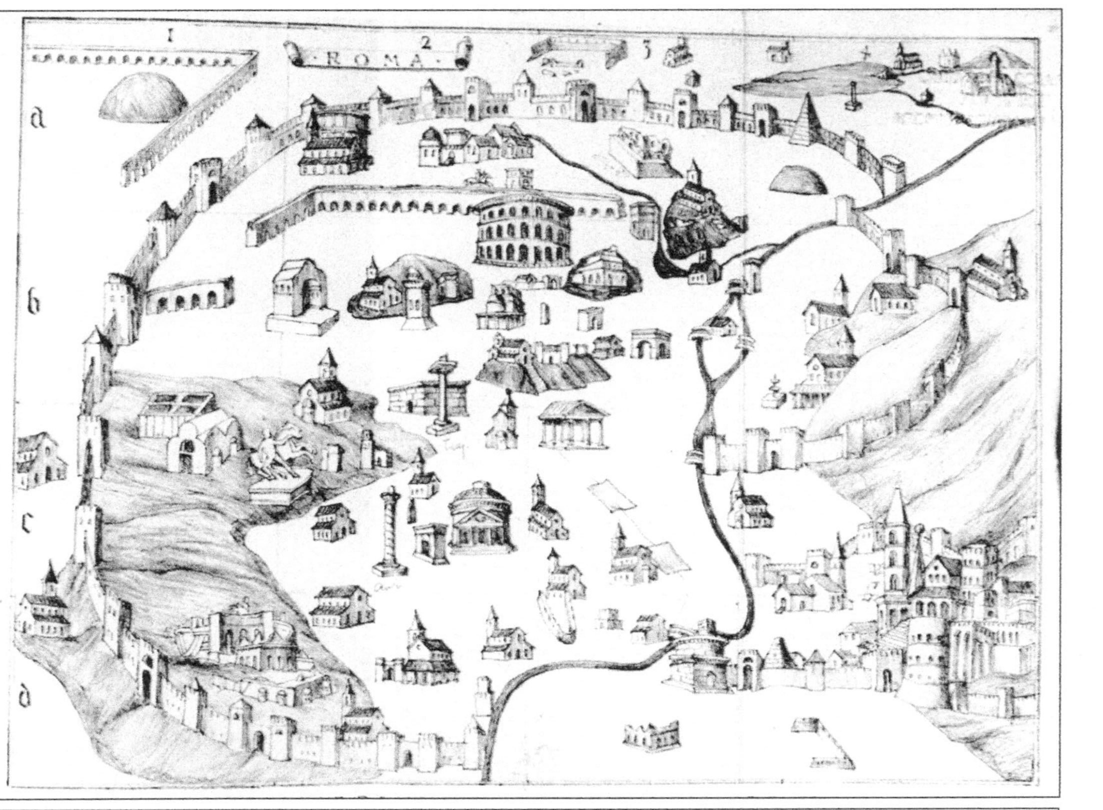

Rome c. 1450.

CONTENTS

PART ONE
The Foundation of Rome and Her Chief Monuments

PART TWO
Famous Places and Images in Rome

PART THREE
A Perambulation of the City

LIST OF ILLUSTRATIONS

PREFACE

THIS EDITION OF THE *MARVELS OF ROME* IS BASED ON AN EDITION PUBLISHED IN ROME AND LONDON IN 1889. FRANCIS MORGAN NICHOLS, ITS TRANSLATOR AND EDITOR, WAS A HISTORIAN WHO DURING HIS CAREER PUBLISHED SEVERAL WORKS ON England and Rome. The text of this edition relies on his translation, although it has been edited and modernized. The aim of this book is to make this fascinating early guide for the traveler and pilgrim to the Eternal City available to the modern reader, traveler and student of Roman history, architecture, and topography.

The *Mirabilia* or *Marvels* was a reliable companion to the city for many centuries. The author was probably Benedict, a canon attached to Saint Peter's, but nothing is known of him except for his great interest in the rebirth of ancient Rome. The guidebook has remained an important source of information on the ancient sites that were still apparent in the medieval city and the names by which they were known.

The work is divided into three parts. The first is a list of the monuments by category, such as the baths or the gates. The second part relates some of the legends that grew up around certain important sites. And the third part resembles a modern guidebook, covering each region and the sites one would see while walking through it. It begins at the Vatican and proceeds to Castel Sant' Angelo before crossing the river to the Mausoleum of Augustus. After leading the pilgrim down through the Campo Marzio toward the Capitoline, the Fora and the Palatine, the guide moves toward the east, the Colosseum and the Circus Maximus; then south to the Caelian and the Lateran; before circling back past the Esquiline and the Aventine. The work finally returns to the Tiber, where it records the sites on the Island and in Trastevere.

One of the major new features of this edition is the Gazetteer, an alphabetical listing of all topographical references that appear in the text. It both locates the structures mentioned in the text and incorporates other information based on, and often including, the notes to the Nichols text. The Gazetteer is arranged alphabetically, except that the churches appear together alphabetically arranged by the Christian name of the saint without considering the form of the adjective "San." The names of all sites referenced in the Gazetteer are capitalized there for easy use.

There are two types of cross-referencing numbers in the Gazetteer. The Arabic numbers in parentheses refer the reader to the part and the chapter of the text where the monument is mentioned. The brackets, which include one Roman number and another number either Roman or Arabic, refer to the location of the monument on the appropriate map after the Gazetteer.

The original Nichols edition contained several other related pieces on Rome, including the *Mirabiliana* and other shorter extracts. These have not been included in this edition, but are referred to in the Gazetteer. The scholarly practices employed by Nichols often made it difficult to verify his references. In those cases the references have been left to stand in the hope that anyone wishing to pursue them further will, at least, be able to retrace as far as Nichols' work. The Preface from the

Nichols edition is reprinted here and changed only slightly to eliminate explanations of his method for indicating sources for different recensions of the text, since this edition silently incorporates material from the three manuscript traditions to establish a more readable text.

Maps, a bibliography and an index have been added to this edition. The five maps reflect both the knowledge of the author about real monuments of the ancient city and the legends attached to many of the unidentified ruins of the medieval city. These maps are therefore as close as possible to the real topography, although some of the monuments shown on them are only conjectural. The bibliography does not aim to be comprehensive but will provide the reader with further sources for study.

PREFACE TO THE FIRST EDITION

THE LITTLE BOOK OF WHICH AN ENGLISH VERSION IS HERE PUBLISHED FOR THE FIRST WAS THE STANDARD GUIDE BOOK OF THE MORE LEARNED VISITORS TO ROME FROM THE TWELFTH TO THE FIFTEENTH CENTURY. ITS STATEMENTS WERE received with the respect due to a work of authority, and their influence may be traced in the writings of many of the authors who flourished during that period. The most striking example of the long-sustained credit of the medieval Roman topography in afforded by the letters of Petrarch. In the descriptions of Rome given by this great leader of the Revival of Learning, scarcely any traces appear of the new critical spirit, but the localities are still presented under the names, and associated with the legends, of the *Mirabilia.*

In the following century, when the wider study of ancient authors and inscriptions had impaired its influence among the learned, the *Mirabilia* still maintained its place in popular estimation; and, after the invention of printing, several editions of it issued forth from the press.

In the present day this treatise is useful to the archeologist as supplying some scanty evidence respecting the history of the sites and buildings of ancient Rome. Under the perplexing veil of an often arbitrary or barbarous nomenclature it exhibits a shadowy picture of the ruins which attracted notice in the medieval city, many of which have since disappeared, while it narrates with charming simplicity the legends with which the principal monuments, and the few works of art which were not buried beneath the surface, were associated in the minds of the more educated people of the time.

It should be added, in estimating the significance of the *Mirabilia,* that the existence and diffusion of the book supply the strongest evidence of the new spirit of curiosity and reverence that had arisen in the twelfth century in regard to the works of ancient art and architecture, which had for many centuries been so ruthlessly destroyed. We should probably not be wrong if we ascribed to this book a powerful influence in the preservation of some at least of the few ruins of importance which still existed in Rome at the time when it was compiled.

Among modern readers, it is not only to the professed archeologist that the *Mirabilia* commends itself. Its delightful legends, and the many natural touches which occur even among the dry lists of gates, arches and ruins, illustrate in the most lively way the manner of thinking which prevailed in the age when it was written, and in the long period during which it continued to be accepted as an authority, when the element of the marvelous maintained so important a place in every department of knowledge. It possesses the same charm as a chapter of the *Travels of Mandeville,* with the advantage that the descriptions have a more solid foundation of fact, and the objects described are to an ordinary educated person more familiar and for the most part more interesting.

Nothing is known concerning the authorship of the book, nor anything of its age or history beyond what may be gathered from the internal evidence of its contents, from the character of the manuscripts in which it has been handed down to us, and from the changes which have at different periods been introduced into its text. For an account of the manuscripts of the *Mirabilia,* the reader may be referred to the critical editions which have been published of the Latin original. It will be sufficient here to give a summary statement of what is known respecting its text.

The earliest extant copy appears to be found in a manuscript of the Vatican Library,[1] attributed to the end of the twelfth century, and in which it is preceded by a list of popes, which ended originally with Celestine III, who ruled from 1191 to 1198, and followed by the chronicle of Romualdus, archbishop of Salerno, ending in the year 1178. Another manuscript of the same library, attributed to the thirteenth century, contains the *Mirabilia* in the same volume with the *Digesta pauperis scholaris Albini,* deacon under Pope Lucius III (1181-85), and with extracts from the *Politicus* of Benedictus Canonicus, written before 1142, and from the writings of Cencius Camerarius, afterward Pope Honorius III (1216-27). The work is found incorporated in other manuscripts with the *Politicus* of Benedictus and with the *Liber Censuum* of Cencius Camerarius. De Rossi[2] has pointed out the importance of this circumstance, not only as bearing upon the question of its age, but also as showing that the *Mirabilia* was about the end of the twelfth century inserted as a quasi-official document among the books of the Roman Curia.

The copies of the *Mirabilia* above referred to exhibit the text in what is regarded as its original form; and it should be observed that the earlier copies have no general title. The name placed upon the title page of this volume is that which was applied to the book in the fourteenth and fifteenth centuries, and by which it has since been generally known.

It appears shortly after its production to have undergone a revision by another hand, which produced a work considerably altered by additions, omissions, and rearrangements of parts. This recension of the *Mirabilia* is distinguished among critics by the name of *Graphia,* because, in a manuscript of the thirteenth or fourteenth century, preserved in the Laurentian Library at Florence, it is found with the title *Graphia aureae urbis Romae.*

With respect to the date of the composition of the *Mirabilia,* we find in the statements of the book itself the following indications, which limit its epoch in one direction. In both forms of the work the porphyry sarcophagus of the emperor Hadrian is described as being at the time the tomb of Innocent II, who died in 1143, and its cover as being in the Parvise of Saint Peter over the prefect's tomb.[3] The prefect has been identified by Gregorovius[4] with the prefect Cinthius or Cencius, who died in 1079. Of a ruin in the Forum, possibly the Temple of Julius, it is said in the earlier work that it is now called the Tower of Cencio Frangipane.[5] This well-known leader in the party warfare of Rome flourished in the early years of the twelfth century.

In the *Graphia* the following references occur, which are not in the original work. The sarcophagus of the empress Helena is said to have been converted into the tomb of Pope Anastasius IV, who died in 1154[6]; and there is mention of a house then belonging to the sons of Pierleone.[7] Pierleone, father of Pope Anaclete II, died in 1128. It is evident from these passages that the *Mirabilia,* it its earliest existing form, is not older than the middle of the twelfth century, to which period it is attributed by some of the best authorities.

Another indication of the date should be mentioned, which, however, is somewhat in controversy. The second, third and fourth chapters of the third part coincide with two sections of the *History of the Basilica of Saint Peter* by Petrus Mallius, a work dedicated to Pope

Alexander III (1159-81).[8] And the question arises to which of the two books these passages originally belonged. The question is discussed by Jordan,[9] who maintains that Mallius borrowed from the *Mirabilia,* while others have assumed the converse to be true. In any case, it appears that the *Mirabilia* should be assigned either to the middle, or the latter half, of the twelfth century, since the age of the earlier manuscripts shows that the work was in existence about the close of that period. Gregorovius, in an interesting account of the *Mirabilia,*[10] dwells upon the allusion to the Palace of the Senators and the Golden Capitol[11] as evidence bearing on the age and suggestive as to the authorship of the book, which he imagines to have been compiled by some one concerned in the revival of the Senate in 1143.

The *Graphia* appears to be of a date not much later than the original work. It is certainly as old as the thirteenth century, its antiquity being confirmed by the fact that Galvaneus Flamma, in a book written in or before 1297, and called *Manipulus Florum,* cites it as *liber valde authenticus.*[12] Martin of Troppau, archbishop of Gnesen (1278), who completed his *Chronicle of the World* in 1268, afterward added an introduction in which he made use if the *Mirabilia* in this form; and Fazio degli Uberti, in his poem called *Il Dittamondo,* written in the meter of the *Divine Comedy* between 1355 and 1367, devotes a canto to a description of Rome in which the poet is evidently largely indebted to the *Graphia.* It was in this form that the *Mirabilia* was known to the English chronicler, Ranulf Higden, who has inserted long extracts from it in that part of the *Polychronicon* which relates to Rome. This work was edited for the Historical Series of the Master of the Rolls by the late Rev. Churchill Babington, who printed with the Latin text two ancient English translations. It is worthwhile to observe that Higden refers to the *Mirabilia Romae* as the work of a certain Magister Gregorius, but the citations appear to be taken from a late revision of the book, and the name Master Gregory does not afford any useful clue to the original authorship.

The *Mirabilia* was first printed in recent times by Montfaucon in 1702 in the *Diarium Italicum.* The manuscript used was then in the Convent of San Isidoro at Rome, and the text appears to be that of the *Graphia* in a late and somewhat enlarged shape. In its older form the Mirabilia was first printed in 1820, from a manuscript attributed to the thirteenth century, then in the Barberini Library, in three several parts of a work called *Effemeridi Litterarie di Roma*[13] with a preface signed by Count Alberti, and with anonymous annotations in Italian, which appear to have been the work of Nibby. This edition was reprinted, with the notes, in a small volume.[14]

The *Mirabilia* was included in two collections of documents published in the same year in Germany and France.[15] I have not seen these collections, but I conclude from the references to them in the editions of Parthey and Urlichs that the former contains the *Mirabilia* in its older form, the latter the *Graphia.* In 1857 the *Mirabilia* was again printed in Germany, in Papencordt's *Geschichte der Stadt Rom im Mittelalter,* edited by Höfler. The text is that of Montfaucon, side by side with another derived from a manuscript at Prague, which appears to belong to the older form of the work. In 1869 Dr. Gustaf Parthey printed the *Mirabilia* at Berlin in an convenient, small octavo volume. His work was the result of a comparison of the text of the Montfaucon with several manuscripts in the Vatican Library with the editions of Alberti and Ozanam. It gives the text of the *Graphia* in a very later form, with some additions found only in one of the Vatican manuscripts.

Professor Henry Jordan, in 1871, published the second volume of his valuable *Topographie der Stadt Rom in Alterthum,* which contains at the end a critical edition of the *Mirabilia,* and in the text a review of its origin and history and a commentary on its contents. In his edition of the text Professor Jordan has taken great pains to distinguish the original composition from the early recension and the additions subsequently made. In the same year Professor Charles Lewis Urlichs published his learned and useful *Codex Urbis Romae Topographicus,* in which he has included the Mirabilia in various successive forms. The first form, which is entitled by the editor *Descriptio plenaria totius urbis,* is what we have described as the original work; the title being taken from one of the Vatican manuscripts already referred to, in which it appears to be applied to the portion of the book called in the English translation the Third Part. The second form is that of the *Graphia.* The third, which he entitles *de mirabilibus civitatis Romae,* resembles the text of Montfaucon. The fourth is the *Mirabilia breviata et interpolata* of the fifteenth century. The fifth is the *Mirabilia cum renascente doctrina coniuncta*; and the sixth is a work founded on the *Mirabilia* and written apparently by a canon of St. Peter's between 1410 and 1415, which was printed by Lewis Merklin in 1852 and is commonly cited by the name of *Anonymous Magliabecchianus,* having been transcribed from a manuscript of the fifteenth century, which has the arms of the Medici at the end and is preserved in the Magliabecchian library in Florence.[16]

The English translation here printed contains the original *Mirabilia,* arranged for the most part in its original order[17]; but the additions of the *Graphia* are introduced into the text, and also such of the later additions of the fourteenth and fifteenth centuries as appear to enhance the value of the work.

The division into chapters is found in several manuscripts but not carried through so completely as it is in the translation. The larger division into parts is not expressly marked in any of the Latin copies but is essential to the arrangement of the matter. Professor Jordan was, I believe, the first to point out that the work in its original form consisted of three distinct portions; first, a list of principal objects of interest arranged under various heads; second, a collection of legends associated with Roman monuments; and third, a sort of perambulation of the ancient city beginning, at the Vatican and ending in Trastevere. In the *Graphia* and later recensions, owing to their deviations from the original arrangement, this division was lost.

Of the notes which have been added, I need not say that they have no pretension to be a complete commentary on the *Mirabilia.* Such a work would occupy a much larger space. They are intended rather to answer the first questions which arise in the mind of the reader to whom the subject is not familiar upon almost every line of this treatise. In their compilation the author has been very largely indebted to the labors of his lamented friend, Professor Henry Jordan, who devoted a considerable part of the second volume of his valuable work on Roman topography, left unfinished at his premature decease, to the illustration of the *Mirabilia.*

— Francis Morgan Nichols
1889

NOTES

1. Cod. Vat. Lat. 3973.
2. De Rossi, *Roma Sotterranea* 1: 158.
3. See below, pp. 36 and 87.
4. 4: 245.
5. See below, pp. 41 and 71.
6. See below, p. 36.
7. See below, p. 45.
8. Printed in volume 27 of the *Acta Sanctorum.*
9. *Topographie Romae* 2: 360, 426.
10. *History of Medieval Rome* 4: 653-65.
11. See below, p. 39.
12. Muratori, *Scriptores* 11: 540.
13. Vol. 1, pp. 62-83, 147-67, 378-92.
14. In 12mo., Rome: Forense, 1864.
15. Grässe, *Beitrage zur Litteratur und Sage des Mittelalters,* 4to., Dresden: 1850; and Ozanam, *Documents inédits pour servir à l'histoire litéraire de l'Italia,* 8to., Paris: 1850.
16. Another copy of this work which appeared to me more carefully written (about the close of the fifteenth century), is in the Library of St. Mark at Venice. MS., Lat. cl. x. cod. 231.
17. The only deviations from the order of the original copies are these: The chapter on Columns (1.10) which is found in those copies among the legends in the Second Part, is placed among the kindred matter of the first part, and the chapter on Holy Places (1.12) is placed at the end of the First Part, instead of preceding that on Bridges. A chapter on the Officers of the Imperial Court, which in some of the earlier copies is inserted in the Second Part, is omitted It is not found in the Vatican manuscript to which the first rank has been assigned.

INTRODUCTION

IN THE TWELFTH CENTURY THE INHABITED PART OF ROME WAS A SMALL CITY TUCKED into the bend of the Tiber River in the midst of the ruins of the great ancient city. The *abitato,* as it was called, extended primarily along the left bank of the river between the Ponte Sant' Angelo and the Tiber Island. The walls and gates of the ancient city were still in place, and between them and the abitato were fields where the animals grazed among the temples and baths, and where monastic houses, great churches, and noble palaces maintained large vineyards, gardens, and farms. Initially the focal point of medieval Rome was the Leonine City, the area around the Castel Sant' Angelo and the Vatican, walled by Pope Leo IV between 847 and 853. The true identity of many of the monuments throughout the rest of the ancient city were lost or forgotten. New names were attached to structures and even to large piles of stones that had never formed a structure. When the function of a structure was in doubt it was often simply called a palace and associated with the name of one of the great emperors.

In the middle of the twelfth century a new interest in the ancient city began to flourish along with the general revival of interest in ancient learning and piety known as the Renaissance of the Twelfth Century. Never a secular movement, this Renaissance looked to the Christian piety of the Apostolic Age and the late Roman Empire for its models. It was an age of religious reform based on a return to the apostolic church; the age of the Waldensians, the Humiliati and the Cathars, of Bernard of Clairvaux, the Cistercians and Carthusians. Yet it was also a sceptical age, the age of Peter Abelard. In the new Gothic art and architecture, Latin and vernacular prose and poetry, the writing of history, philosophy, law and science, scholars and artists sought new sources of inspiration or information. Scholars began to seek out ancient manuscripts or to translate those long available to the Greek and Moslem worlds. The new learning soon left the monastic and cathedral schools and gave birth to Europe's first universities, where Logic became queen and replaced literary discourse as the chief tool of inquiry in both philosophy and theology.

This Renaissance coincided with a new age of political consolidation and economic expansion, of increased stability and wealth, of wider trade and travel. It also witnessed the the rise of the new Italian communes. These sworn associations of largely "patrician" and merchant families overthrew the rule of feudal and church overlords to set up independent city–states. This soon led to their conscious revival of Roman Law and civic institutions, as the office of *consul* began to spread throughout the peninsula and the new urban democracies began to look for legal and historical precedents for their revolutionary institutions.

At the same time the twelfth century witnessed a series of "second" popes. Urban II, Paschal II, Innocent II and Anacletus II all call to mind strong-willed men bent on the reform of religious life and the centralized control of the church under the Roman pontiff. The names they picked consciously recalled the popes and martyrs of the first great age of Christian Rome. The builders of the new churches turned to the Roman ruins for ideas and inspiration and even for the building materials themselves. Columns and pillars were moved from their former sites to hold up the roofs of the new churches. From outside Rome artists, architects, and writers began to make their way to Rome to look for inspiration too. Elaborate plans were even devised for transporting Roman columns to support the roof of Saint Denis, the burial church of the French kings outside Paris.

A revival of trade and travel across the Mediterranean to the Holy Land, North Africa, and the lands beyond in the twelfth century precipitated a great period of travel literature and guidebooks. Another major factor that contributed to this literary phenomenon was the new popularity of pilgrimages, as waves of the devout and curious made their way to Palestine or to the sacred sites of Europe to retrace the steps of Christ, the Apostles, and the saints. The guidebooks exhibited a revival of much of the learning of antiquity — mixed with new legends — and the absorption of Greek and Islamic geographical knowledge through many translations. Finally, the revival of Italian urban life had sparked a new pride of place and a new interest in researching and describing the ancient traditions, monuments, topography, and events of the Italian cities. Finding ancient Roman foundations thus lent legitimacy to the new democratic states and helped highlight both the new building and the restoration of ancient sites and political institutions.

At this time there were also political changes occurring within Rome itself. In 1142 the Romans rose up against Pope Innocent II (1130–43) and reestablished the Roman Senate. In 1145 they welcomed to the city the great reformer and critic of clerical corruption, Arnold of Brescia. For nearly a decade Rome remained divided between the Leonine City, held by the popes, and the *abitato.* Thus, when the ancient Senate was reestablished on the Capitoline, the focus of the city began to shift physically toward the area of the ancient imperial Fora and mentally toward the ancient glory of the city and the power of its citizens, senators and consuls. While Arnold's career was to end on the heretic's pyre and Rome itself was to be torn in bloody battle between the Roman commune and the forces of the Holy Roman Emperor, Frederick I Barbarossa, the sense survived among the Romans themselves that they were living in the revived capitol of the ancient world.

At about this time the *Mirabilia Urbis Romae* appeared, written around 1143 by a canon of St. Peter's named Benedict. It was probably the most influential guide for the traveler and pilgrim to the sites of the city. Yet the churches of Rome and other contemporary sites serve characteristically as merely locators for the ancient monuments. The early Christian legends, which are related in the second part of the guide, often focus more on the nobility of the Roman citizens and their senators and consuls than on the religious fervor of the martyrs. The guide aims less to infuse the pilgrim with religious fervor, than to point out the temples and palaces and thus "to bring back to the human memory how great was their beauty in gold, silver, brass, ivory and precious stones."

It is, then, one of the distinctive features of the *Mirabilia* to bring together so many of the characteristics of the Twelfth Century Renaissance. The book is a guide for the devout pilgrim seeking to retrace the footsteps of Peter and Paul and the other Christian martyrs. It is a paean to the monuments of Roman civic life: the Senate and Capitoline, the walls and towers, the public temples, baths and tombs of the emperors. It is also a learned treatise on the historical traditions of the city itself, of its art and architecture. It is thus a synthesis of the acts of the Roman emperors and of the Christian martyrs reflected daily in the very fabric of Rome's crowded churches and its grand — if desolate — ruins.

— Eileen Gardiner

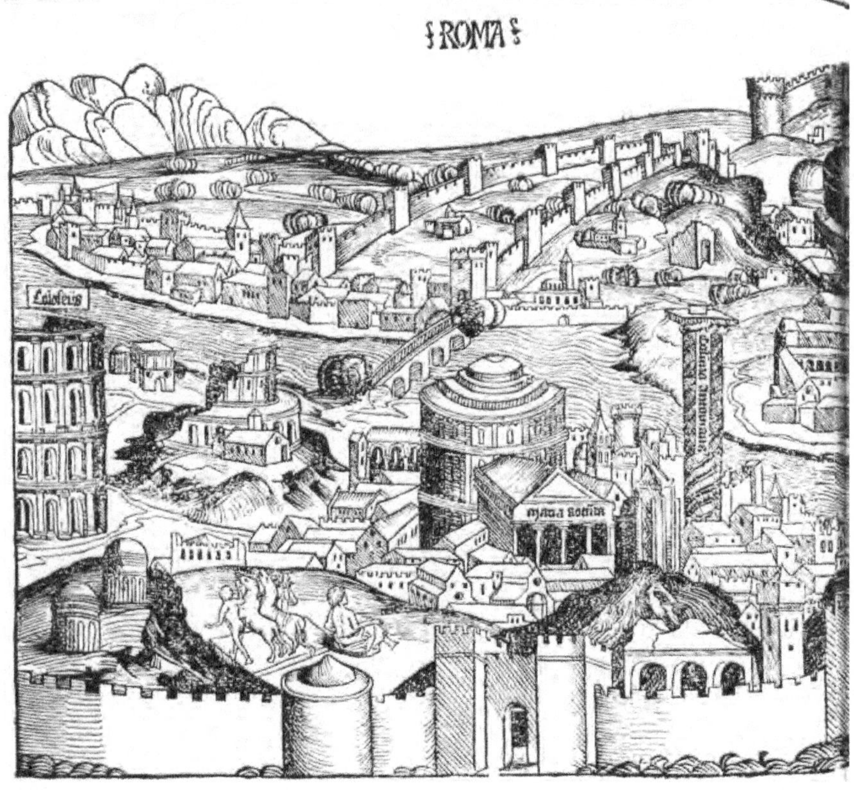

Rome c. 1493

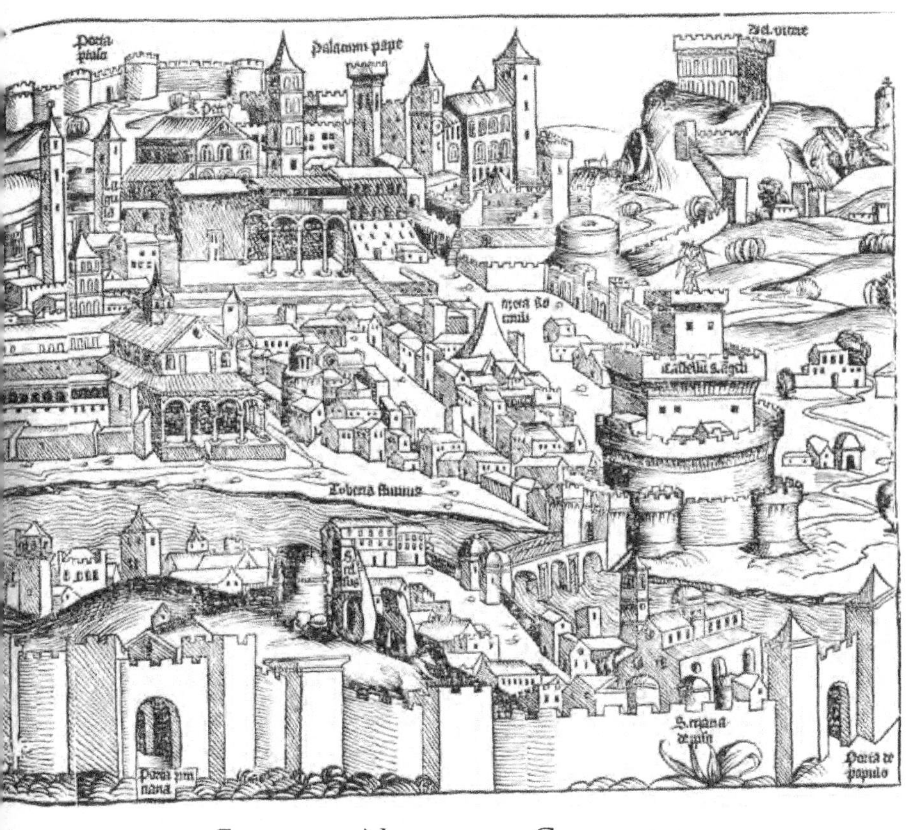

From the Nuremberg Chronicle

PART ONE

The Foundation of Rome

Her Wall, Gates, Arches, Hills, Baths,
Palaces, Theaters, Bridges,
Pillars, Cemeteries
and
Holy Places

I

The Foundation of Rome

After the Sons of Noah built the Tower of Confusion, Noah with his sons boarded a ship, as Hescondius writes, and came to Italy. Not far from the place where Rome is now he founded a city in his own name where he ended his suffering and his life. Then his son Janus, with Janus his son, Japhet his grandson and Camese, a man of the country, built a city, Janiculum on the Palatine Hill, and took over the kingdom. When Camese died the kingdom passed to Janus alone. He, with Camese, built a palace in Trastevere, which he called Janiculum, where the Church of San Giovanni in Janiculum now stands. But he had the seat of his kingdom in the palace, which he had built on the Palatine Hill where afterwards all the emperors and Caesars gloriously dwelt. Moreover at that time Nembroth, who is the same as Saturnus, who was shamefully treated by his son Jupiter, came to the realm of Janus and, supported by his aid, Saturnus founded a city on the Capitoline, which he called Saturnia after himself.

In those days King Italus with the Syracusans, coming to Janus and Saturnus, built a city by the River Albula, and named it after him, and the River Albula they named

Tiber after the dike of Syracuse. After this Hercules with the Argives came to the realm of Janus, as Varro tells, and founded a city called Valentia under the Capitoline. And afterwards, Tibris, king of the Aborigines, came with his nation and built a city by the Tiber, near where he was slain by Italus in a fight. Evander, king of Arcadia, with his people built a city on the Palatine. Coribas came with a host of Sicanians and built a city close by in the valley. And also Glaucus, younger son of the son of Jupiter, came with his people, raised a city and built walls. Then Roma, the daughter of Aeneas, came with a multitude of Trojans and built a city in the palace of the town. Aventinus Silvius, king of the Albans, erected a palace and mausoleum on the Aventine Hill for himself.

Finally four hundred and thirty-three years after the destruction of Troy, Romulus was born of the blood of Priam, king of the Trojans. At the age of twenty-two, on the fifteenth day of the Calends of May, Romulus enclosed all these cities with a wall and called the place Rome after himself. And in Rome Etrurians, Sabines, Albans, Tusculans, Politanes, Telenes, Ficanians, Janiculans, Camerians, Capenates, Faliscans, Lucanians, Italians, and, as it could be said, all the noble men of the whole earth, with their wives and children, came together to dwell here.

II

The Town Wall

The wall of the city of Rome has three hundred sixty-one towers, forty-nine castles, seven major arches, six thousand nine hundred battlements, twelve gates, five posterns, and is twenty-two miles around, without counting in Trastevere and the Leonine City, which is the same as Saint Peter's Porch.

III

The Gates

The gates of the famous city are these: the Porta Capena, which is now called Porta San Paolo, near the Temple of Remus; Porta Appia, at the Church of Domine Quo Vadis, or "Lord, where are you going?," where the footsteps of Jesus Christ are seen; Porta Latina, because there the Latins and Apulians used to go into the city; there is a vessel here that was filled with boiling oil and in which the Blessed John the Evangelist was set; Porta Metronia; Porta Asinaria, which is called the Lateran Gate; Porta Labicana, which is called Porta Maggiore; Porta Taurina, which is called Porta San Lorenzo or the Gate of Tivoli and it is called *Taurina* or the Bull Gate because there are carved on it two heads of bulls, one of them lean and the other fat. The lean head on the outside signifies those who come with slender means into the city; the fat and full head on the inside signifies those who leave the city rich; Porta Nomentana, which leads to the city of Nomentum; Porta Salaria, which leads into two roads, one the old Via Salaria that leads to the Ponte Milvio and the new way that goes to the Ponte Salaria; Porta Pinciana named because King Pincius had his palace there; Porta Flaminia, which is called San Valentino; Porta Collina at the castle that is near Saint Peter's Bridge, which is called the Emperor Hadrian's Castle. He also made Saint Peter's Bridge.

Beyond the Tiber there are three gates: Porta Septimiana, seven Naiads joined with Janus; Porta Aurelia or aurea, that is to say golden, which is now called Porta San Pancrazio; and Porta Portese. There are two gates in Saint Peter's Porch. One is the Porta Castel Sant' Angelo and the other Porta Viridaria or the gate at the garden.

IV

The Triumphal Arches

The triumphal arches are these that follow, which were made for emperors returning from triumphs and which they were led under with worship by the senators, and the victory was carved on the arch as a memorial for posterity: Alexander's Golden Arch at Saint Celsus, the Arch of the Emperors Theodosius and Valentinian and Gratian at Sant' Urso; the triumphal arch of marble that the Senate decreed was to be adorned with trophies in honor of Drusus, the father of Claudius Caesar, because of his noble handling of the Rhaetic and German wars, although the vestiges now are barely visible outside the Appian Gate at the Temple of Mars; in the Circus the Arch of Titus and Vespasian; the Arch of Constantine near the Amphitheater; at Santa Maria Nova between the Greater Palace and the Temple of Romulus, the Arch of the Seven Lamps of Titus and Vespasian where is found Moses' candlestick with seven branches with the Ark, at the foot of the Cartulary Tower; the Arch of Julius Caesar and the Senators between the Temple of Concord and the Fatal Temple, before Santa Martina, where the Breeches Towers are now; near San Lorenzo in Lucina, the triumphal Arch of Octavian; the Arch of

Antoninus, near his pillar, where the Tower of the Tosetti is now.

Then there is the Arch at San Marco, called Hand of Flesh, for at the time in Rome when Lucy, a holy matron, was tormented for the faith of Christ by the Emperor Diocletian, he commanded that she should be laid down and beaten to death. The man who struck her, however, was turned to stone, but his hand remained flesh for seven days, so the place is called Hand of Flesh to this day. On the Capitoline is the Arch of the Gold Bread; and on the Aventine the Arch of Faustinus near Santa Sabina.

There are, moreover, other arches, which are not triumphal but memorial arches, such as the Arch of Piety in front of Santa Maria Rotonda. In this place at one time, when an emperor [Trajan] was prepared to go forth to war in his chariot, a poor widow fell at his feet, weeping and crying, "Oh my lord, before you go, let me have justice." And he promised her that on his return he would do her full right, but she said, "Perhaps you shall die first." Considering this the emperor leaped from his chariot and held his consistory on the spot. And the woman said, "I had only one son and a young man has killed him." When he heard this the emperor gave his sentence. "The murderer," he said, "shall die; he shall not live." "Your son then," she said, "shall die, for it is he who while playing with my son has slain him." But when he was led to death the woman sighed aloud and said, "Let the young man who is to die be given to me in place of my son. So shall I be repayed, or else I shall never agree that I have had full justice." This therefore was done, and the woman departed with rich gifts from the emperor.

V

The Hills

These are the hills within the city: the Janiculum, commonly called the Janarian; where the Church of Santa Saba is, the Aventine, which is also called the Quirinal because the Quirites were there, where the Church of Sant' Alessio is; the Caelian where the Church of Santo Stefano in Monte Caelio is; the Capitoline or the Tarpeian Hill, where the Senators' Palace is; the Palatine where the Greater Palace is; the Esquiline which is called the highest, where the Basilica of Santa Maria Maggiore is; the Viminal where the Church of Sant' Agata is and where Virgil, being taken by the Romans, escaped invisibly and went to Naples, whence it is said, *"vado ad Napulim."*

VI

The Baths

There are great palaces called baths with large underground crypts, where in the winter a fire was kindled throughout. In summer the crypts were filled with fresh waters so the court could dwell in the upper chambers in much delight. These crypts may be seen in the Baths of Diocletian in front of the Church of Santa Susanna. There are also the Baths of Antoninus, the

Baths of Domitian, the Maximian, those of Licinius, the Baths of Diocletian, the Baths of Tiberius behind Santa Susanna; the Novatian; those of Olympias at San Lorenzo in Panisperna; those of Agrippa behind Santa Maria Rotonda; and the Alexandrine near the hospital of the baths.

VII

The Palaces

These are the Palaces of the city. There is the Greater Palace of the monarchy of the earth, the capital seat of the whole world, and the Caesarean Palace on the Palatine Hill; the Palace of Romulus near the hut of Faustulus; the Palace of Severus by San Sisto; the Palace of Claudius between the Colosseum and San Pietro in Vincoli; the Palace of Constantine in the Lateran, where my lord the pope dwells. This Lateran Palace was Nero's and named either for the side of the northern region where it stands or from the frog that Nero secretly produced. In this palace there is now a great church. There is the Susurrian Palace where now the Church of Santa Croce is; the Volusian Palace; the Palace of Romulus between Santa Maria Nova and San Cosma, where there are the two Temples of Piety and Concord, and where Romulus set his golden image saying: "It shall not fall until a virgin bears a child." And as soon as the Virgin bore a son, the image fell down.

There is the Palace of Trajan and Hadrian, where there is the pillar twenty paces of height; Constantine's Palace; the Palace of Sallust; the Palace of Camillus; the Palace of Antoninus, where his pillar stands twenty-seven paces high; Nero's Palace where Saint Peter's Needle is and where the bodies of the Apostles Peter and Paul, Simon and Jude rest; Julius Caesar's Palace, where the Sepulcher of Julius Caesar is found; the Palace of Chromatius; the Palace of Euphimianus; the Palace of Titus and Vespasian outside Rome at the catacombs; Domitian's Palace beyond the Tiber in Mica Aurea and Octavian's Palace at San Lorenzo in Lucina.

VIII

The Theaters

There are these theaters: Titus and Vespasian's Theater at the catacombs; the Theater of Tarquin and the Emperors at the Septizonium; Pompey's Theater at San Lorenzo in Damaso; the Theater of Antoninus by the Bridge of Antoninus; Alexander's Theater near Santa Maria Rotonda; Nero's Theater near the Castle of Crescentius; and the Flaminian Theater.

IX

The Bridges

These are the bridges: the Milvian Bridge; Hadrian's Bridge; the Neronian Bridge in Sassia; the Bridge of Antoninus in Arenula; the Fabrician Bridge, which is called the Jew's Bridge, because Jews dwell there; Gratian's Bridge between the island and

Trastevere; the Senator's Bridge of Santa Maria; the marble Bridge of Theodosius at the Riparmea, and the Valentinian Bridge.

X

The Pillars of Antoninus and Trajan, and the Ancient Images of Rome

The winding pillar of Antoninus is one hundred seventy-five feet high, has two hundred and three steps and forty-five windows. The winding Pillar of Trajan is one hundred thirty-eight feet high, one hundred eighty-five steps and has forty-five windows. The colossal Amphitheater is about one hundred eight submissal feet high.

In Rome were twenty-two great horses of gilded brass, eighty horses of gold, eighty-four horses of ivory, one hundred eighty-four public privies, fifty great sewers; bulls, griffins, peacocks and a multitude of other images, the costliness of which seemed so beyond measure that people who came to the city had good reason to marvel at Rome's beauty.

XI

The Cemeteries

These are Rome's cemeteries: at San Pancrazio the Cemetery of Calepodius, the Cemetery of Sant' Agata ad Girolum, the Cemetery of Urso at Portesa, the Cemetery of San Felice, the Cemetery of Callisto by the catacombs at the Church of Santi Fabiano and Sebastiano; the Cemetery of Praetextatus near the Appian Gate at Sant' Apollinare; Gordian's Cemetery outside the Porta Latina; the Cemetery between Two Bays at Saint Helena's; the Cemetery of the Capped Bear at Santa Viviana; the Cemetery of the *Ager Veranus* at San Lorenzo fuori le Mura; the Cemetery of Sant' Agnese; the Cemetery of Saint Peter's Well; Cemetery of Priscilla at the Salarian Bridge; the Cemetery at the Cucumber Hill; Traso's Cemetery at San Saturnino; the Cemetery of Santa Felicità near that of Callisto; the Cemetery of San Marcello on the old Via Salaria; the Cemetery of Balbina on the Via Ardeatina; the Cemetery of the Innocenti at San Paolo; the Pontian Cemetery; the Cemetery of Santi Ermio and Domitilla; the Cemetery of San Cyriaco on the Via Ostiense. These cemeteries were chambers underground that sometimes stretched for three miles and where the holy martyrs were hidden.

XII

The Places of Martyrdom

These are the places that are found in the Passions

Passions of the Saints: outside the Porta Appia, the place where the Blessed Sixtus was beheaded and the place where the Lord appeared to Peter when he said, "Lord, where are you going?" and the Temple of Mars; inside the gate the Arch of Drusus; then, the region of Fasciola at San Nereo; the *Vicus Canarius* at San Giorgio, where Lucilla's house was and where the Golden Vail is; the Acqua Salvia at Sant' Anastasio where Saint Paul was beheaded and his head uttered the word "Jesus" three times as it bounded, and where there are still three wells that sprang up, each one different in taste; the Garden of Lucina, where the Church of San Paolo fuori le Mura stands and where Saint Paul's body lies. *Interlude,* that is, between two games; the Hill of Scaurus, which is between the Colosseum and the Circus Maximus before the Septizonium, where the sewer is into which Saint Sebastian was cast, who revealed his body to Saint Lucina, saying, "You shall find my body hanging on a nail." The Via Cornelia is near the Ponte Milvio and goes into the street; the Via Aurelia near the Circus of Caligula; the steps of Eliogabalus at the entry of the Palace; the chained island behind Santa Trinità; the Arch of Drusus before the Septizonium; the Roman Arch between the Aventine and Albiston where Saint Silvester and Constantine kissed and departed from each other; in *Tellure,* that is the

Cannapara, where the house of Tellus was; the Mamertine Prison before the Mars under the Capitoline; the Vicus Latericii at Santa Prasede; the *Vicus Patricii* at Santa Prudenziana; the Basilica of Jupiter at San Quirico; the Baths of Olympias where Saint Laurence was broiled, in Panisperna; the Tiberian Palace of Trajan where Decius and Valerian went after Saint Laurence's death, at the Baths of the Cornuti; the Circus Flaminius at the Jews' Bridge; in Trastevere, the Temple of the Ravennates pouring forth oil at Santa Maria in Trastevere.

PART TWO

FAMOUS PLACES AND IMAGES IN ROME

The Legends Behind Rome's Monuments

I

The Vision of Octavian and the Sibyl's Answer

In the time of Emperor Octavian the Senators seeing him to be of such great beauty that none could look into his eyes and of such great prosperity and peace that he made all the world render tribute to him, said to him, "We desire to worship you because the godhead is in you; for if it were not so all things would not prosper with you as they do." But he was reluctant and demanded a delay and called the Sibyl of Tibur to him, and he repeated all that the senators had said. She begged for three days time, during which she kept a strict fast, and then answered him after the third day. "These things, lord emperor, shall surely come to pass:

> Token of doom: the earth shall drip with sweat;
> From heaven shall come the king for evermore,
> And present in the flesh shall judge the world."

And the other verses that follow. And while Octavian diligently listened to the Sibyl, heaven opened, and a great brightness shone on him, and he saw in heaven a virgin exceedingly fair standing on an altar holding a man-child in her arms. Octavian marveled greatly at this, and he heard a voice from heaven saying: "This is the Virgin who shall conceive the Savior of the World." And again he heard another voice from heaven saying, "This is the altar of the Son of God." The emperor straightway fell to the ground and worshipped the Christ that should come. He showed this vision to the senators and they likewise marveled exceedingly. The vision took place in the chamber of Emperor Octavian where the Church of Santa Maria in Capitolio is now and where the Friars Minor are. Therefore it is called Santa Maria in Aracoeli.

Another day when the people had decreed to call Octavian "Lord," he immediately stopped them with his gesture and glance. He did not allow himself to be called "Lord" even by his sons saying: "Mortal I am and [you] will not call me Lord."

II

The Dioscuri

Hear now why the horses of marble were made bare and the men beside them naked, and what story they tell, and also why before the horses sits a certain woman encompassed with serpents and with a shell in front of her.

In the time of Emperor Tiberius two young men who were philosophers, named Praxiteles and Phidias, came to Rome. Since the emperor noticed that they had so much wisdom, he kept them near him in his palace, and he said to them, "Why do you go about naked?" They answered and said, "Because all things are naked and open to us. We hold the world of no account, therefore we go naked and possess nothing." They also said, "Whatever you, most mighty emperor, shall devise in your chamber by day or night, although we are not there, we will tell you every word." "If you do as you say, " said the emperor, "I will give you whatever you desire." They answered and said, "We ask no money but only a memorial of us." And when the next day came they repeated to the emperor, in order, whatever he thought of during that night. Therefore he made them the memorial that he had promised, that is, the naked horses, which trample on the earth, that is on the mighty princes of the world that rule over the men of this world. And there shall come a very mighty king who shall mount the horses, that is, upon the might of the princes of this world.

Meanwhile there are the two men half-naked, who stand by the horses with their arms raised high and with fingers bent who tell of the things that are to be, and they are naked as all worldly knowledge is naked and open to their minds. The woman encompassed with serpents, who sits with a shell before her signifies the church, encompassed with many rolls of scriptures, but whoever desires to go to her may not unless first washed in that shell, that is, unless baptized.

III

Constantine's Horse

At the Lateran there is a certain bronze horse called Constantine's Horse, but it is not so. Whoever will know the truth, let him read it here.

Miribilia Urbis Romae

In the time of the consuls and senators a certain very mighty king from the East came to Italy and beseiged Rome on the side of the Lateran, and with much slaughter and war afflicted the Roman people. Then a certain squire, very handsome and virtuous, bold and clever, arose. He said to the consuls and senators, "If there were one who should deliver you from this tribulation, what would he deserve from the Senate?" They answered, "Whatever he shall ask he shall immediately have." "Give me," he said, "thirty thousand sesterces, and you shall make me a memorial of the victory when the fight is done and a horse of the best gilded brass." And they promised to do all that he asked. Then he said, "Arise at midnight and arm yourselves and stand watch within the walls, and whatever I say, you do." And they did as he told them.

Then he mounted a horse without a saddle and took a sickle. He had seen on many nights the king come to the foot of a certain tree for his bodily need. At his coming an owlet, who sat in the tree, always hooted. The squire therefore went out of the city and gathered forage, which he carried in front of him tied up in a truss in the manner of a groom. And as soon as he heard the hooting of the owlet he drew near and saw that the king had come to the tree. He therefore went straight toward him. The lords who were with the king thought the squire was one of their own people and began to cry that he should get away from the king. But he did not give up his purpose on account of their shouting. He feigned to move away but instead he bore down on the king. Such was his boldness that in spite of them all he seized the king by force and carried him away. When he was at the walls of the city he began to cry, "Go forth and slay all the king's army. See, I have taken the king captive." And they sallied out and slew some and put others to flight.

The Romans took an untold quantity of silver and gold from that field. They returned glorious to the city, and all that they had promised to the squire they paid and performed. They gave him thirty thousand sesterces and made the horse of gilded brass without a saddle as a memorial of him. The man himself rides thereon, stretching out his right hand, with which he took the king. As a memorial on the horse's head is the owlet whose hooting won the squire his victory. The king, who was of small stature, with his hands bound behind him, as he was captured, was also depicted, as a memorial, under the hoof of the horse.

IV

The Pantheon

In the times of the senators and consuls the Prefect Agrippa with four legions of soldiers subjugated the Suevians, Saxons and other western nations to the Roman Senate. The bell of the image of the kingdom of the Persians, which was on the Capitoline, rang when he returned. In the Temple of Jupiter and Moneta on the Capitoline was an image of every kingdom of the world with a bell about its neck, and as soon as the bell sounded they knew that the country was rebellious. The priest who was on watch that week, hearing the sound of the bell, therefore showed it to the senators. The senators gave the Prefect Agrippa responsibility for organizing this war. He initially denied that he was able to carry out so great a charge, but he was at length compelled, and he then asked permission to take counsel for three days.

During this period, one night, after too much thinking, he fell asleep, and there appeared to him a woman who said to him, "What are you doing, Agrippa? You are very deep in thought." He answered her, "Madam, I am." She said, "Comfort yourself and promise me if you shall win the victory to make me a temple such as I will show you." And he said, "I will make it." And she showed him in a vision a temple made after that fashion. And he said, "Madam, who are you?" And she said, "I am Cybele, the mother of the gods. Bear libations to Neptune, who is a mighty god, so that he will help you and have this temple dedicated to my worship and Neptune's, because we will be with you, and you shall prevail."

Agrippa then arose with gladness and repeated in the Senate all of this conversation. He then went with a great array of ships and with five legions and overcame the Persians and put them under a yearly tribute to the Roman Senate. When he returned to Rome he built this temple and had it dedicated to the honor of Cybele, mother of the gods, and to the honor of Neptune, god of the sea, and to the honor of all the gods, and he called this temple the Pantheon. In honor of the same Cybele he made a gilded image, which he set upon the top of the temple above the opening and covered it with a magnificant roof of gilded brass.

After many ages Pope Boniface, in the time of Phocas, a Christian emperor, seeing that such a marvelous temple, dedicated to the honor of Cybele, mother of the gods, before which Christian people were often stricken by devils, prayed to the emperor to grant this temple to him so that, as it was dedicated to Cybele, mother of the gods, on the Calends of November, he might consecrate it to the Blessed Mary, ever-virgin, who is the mother of all the saints, on the Calends of November. Caesar granted this to him, and the pope with the whole Roman people on the Calends of November dedicated the temple and ordained that on that day the Roman pontiff should sing mass there, and the people should take the body and blood of Our Lord as they did on Christmas. On the same day all the saints with their mother, Mary ever-virgin, and the heavenly spirits should have a festival, and throughout the churches of the world the dead would have a sacrifice for the ransom of their souls.

V

The Passions of Saints Abdon and Sennen, Sixtus and Laurence

One approach for preaching the passions of Saint Abdon and Saint Sennen, or Saint Sixtus, Saint Laurence and the rest would, as the legend relates, examine why the emperor put them to death and would begin thus: "After a tempest arose under Decius, many Christians were slain, while Galba ruled in the city of Rome."

The other approach, as the Roman legend relates, would begin like this and preach: "There was a certain emperor, Gordian by name, whose standard-bearer in the legions was Philip. Philip was a Christian, and he slew his lord the Emperor Gordian and took the empire with his son, for he had a son named Philip. Now among the servants of the Emperor Philip there was a certain knight named Decius, a heathen man of Pannonia, who gained the favor of the emperor by the good reputation of his knighthood and of the soldiers and the Senate by his wit, prudence and bounty. The emperor with the Senate made him chief captain with four legions against a nation of the West that was rebellious. Decius went and made war against them and overcame them in many battles. When he returned his soldiers, rejoicing, praised him and said, "Oh, if he were our emperor all things would be well with us."

Being tempted by the soldiers' words, he conspired with them to have the empire and promised to give them duchies and marches and counties and honors at court and the treasure of Philip. Now when Decius reached the region of Liguria, the Emperor Philip had moved to Verona, and when he heard of the return of Decius he received him graciously. But after that day had passed the soldiers of Decius secretly took up arms, as they had agreed with their emperor-to-be, and Decius at noon went to the emperor's court with a concealed sword, and entering the emperor's tent, he cast out his attendant and drawing his sword struck Philip between the nose and the lip as he slept in his bed and so killed him. Then Decius went forth and sounded a signal, whereupon all his soldiers ran to meet him around the tent, as they had devised beforehand. Meanwhile Philip's soldiers heard that their lord was slain by Decius and they fled, but they were called back in their terror by Decius, who told them not to flee but to become his friends. They finally did return to him, but from fear rather than from love.

Now when the younger Philip, who was at Rome, heard that his father, Philip, was murdered by Decius the pagan, he was afraid and fled to the Blessed Sixtus, pope of the Romans, saying, "My lord Father, my father is dead. The impious Decius murdered him. I beg you to take my father's treasure and keep it hidden. If I escape, and Decius does not kill me, you shall give it back to me again, but if not you shall have it for the church. Decius then came to Rome and took over the empire more by his valor than because of any love that was borne him. He began to seek Philip the Younger who was hidden away. At last, after great promises and gifts, he found him and murdered him. Then he searched for the treasure of Philip. Some said that Sixtus, the pope of the Christians, had it. Others said that is was at Philippopolis in Greece.

At this very same time an embassy came from the ruler of Persia saying that the Persians were rebelling, and the bell of the image rang. Decius, therefore, appointed Galba to be his vicar at Rome and brought his son Decius with him and fought against the Persians and conquered them all. At this time he took Abdon and Sennen, as the legend tells, whom he knew to be of a noble race, and he brought them away chained in golden fetters. As Decius returned he laid seige to Philippopolis. In the meantime a message came from Rome bringing him news that Galba was dead. So he left Decius, his son, there with a part of his army and led the rest to Rome together with Abdon and Sennen.

Now, when he had arrived in Rome he asked diligently after the treasures of Philip, which he had not yet been able to find. He also slew those holy martyrs, the very noble Abdon and Sennen, in the Colosseum. And it was shown to him that Sixtus, bishop of the Christians, had the treasure of Philip, so he took Sixtus and tortured him. But because Sixtus would not assure him about the treasures, Valerian commanded that Sixtus should be sentenced to death. As Sixtus was led to be beheaded, the Blessed Laurence cried out and said, "Holy Father, do not leave me behind, for I have spent the treasures that you put into my hands." Then the soldiers, hearing of the treasures, laid hands on the Blessed Laurence before the Seven Floors of the New Way and took him and delivered him to Parthenius the tribune: and the rest that follows.

VI

Octavian and the Church of San Pietro in Vincoli

When Julius Caesar was assassinated by the Senate, his nephew Octavian took up the rule of the empire. Antony, his brother-in-law, who had remained in power after Caesar's death, rose against him. He strove with much effort to take the empire from him. Antony, therefore, divorced Octavian's sister, took as a wife Cleopatra, queen of Egypt, wealthy in gold and silver, precious stones and people. When Antony and Cleopatra began to move against Rome with a great array of ships and people, the news was brought to Rome. Octavian with a mighty force went and fought against them in Epirus. A battle began, and the queen's ship, which was all gilded, began to give way. Antony saw the queen's ship give way and also withdrew and followed her to Alexandria, where he fell on his sword and died. After this Queen Cleopatra saw that she was reserved for a triumph, so she decked herself with gold and precious stones and tried to bewitch Octavian with her beauty, but she could not. Finding herself scorned, she went as she was into her husband's tomb and put to her breasts two asps, which is a kind of serpent. They sucked so sweetly that she fell asleep and died.

Octavian took away vast sums of money from that victory and triumphed over Alexandria and Egypt and all the country of the East and so came back to Rome victorious. The Senate and all the Roman people received him with great triumph, and because his victory was on the Calends of the month Sextilis, they gave him the name of Augustus because of the augment or increase of the state and decreed that every year on the Calends of August, for so they also called the month, the whole commonwealth should have a festival of gladness commemorating this victory in honor of Octavianus Caesar Augustus, and the whole city should rejoice and be glad in this great festival.

This rite endured to the time of Arcadius, the husband of Eudoxia, who after his death was left with her young son Theodosius and ruled the empire as a man, as though her husband Arcadius were still alive. Moved by the spirit of God, and for the welfare of the commonwealth, she went to Jerusalem and visited the holy places. While she was busy with the affairs of the commonwealth the provincial folk brought her huge gifts. A certain Jew brought her the chains of the Blessed Apostle Peter with which he was bound by Herod in prison under four quaternions. The sight of these chains gave the queen more joy than all her other gifts, and she thought that they could not be put in a more worthy place than where the Blessed Peter's body rests in dust.

Coming to Rome on the Calends of August she saw that ancient rite of heathendom still full solemnly observed by the Roman people on the Calends of Sextilis, which none of the pontiffs had been able to discontinue. She, therefore, appealed to Pope Pelagius and the senators and the people, and asked that the favor that she sought might be granted to her. They readily promised to allow it. The queen therefore said, "I do not perceive that you give much thought to the Sextile holiday in reverence of the dead Emperor Octavian and his victory over the Egyptians. I pray you give up the worship of the dead Emperor Octavian for the worship of the heavenly Emperor and his Apostle Peter, whose chains, you see, I have brought from Jerusalem. Just as Octavian delivered us from Egyptian bondage, so did the heavenly Emperor deliver us from the bondage of demons. I intend to build a church to God's honor and to Saint Peter's and to set these chains there. The pope, our lord apostolic, shall dedicate this church on the Calends of August, and it shall be called San Pietro in Vincoli. There every year our apostolic lord shall sing solemn mass in the same church, and as Saint Peter was freed by the angel, so may the Roman people depart with a blessing, freed from their sins."

This proposal was heard by the people and received with little favor but was at length granted according to the prayer of the pope and the queen. She therefore built the church, which the pope dedicated on the Calends of August, as the most Christian empress had devised. There she set the chains of the Blessed Peter and the Neronian chains of the Blessed Paul. To this day on the Calends of Sextilis the Roman people may flock there and do reverence to the chains of the Apostles Peter and Paul.

VII

The Colosseum

The Colosseum was the Temple of the Sun. It was of marvelous beauty and greatness, disposed with many different vaulted chambers and all covered with a heaven of gilded brass, where thunder and lightning and glittering fire were made, and where rain was shed through slender tubes. Besides this there were the supercelestial signs and the planets *Sol* and *Luna,* which were drawn along in their proper chariots. And in the middle dwelled Phoebus, who is the god of the Sun. With his feet on the earth he reached to heaven with his head and held in his hand an orb that signified that Rome ruled over the whole world.

After some time the Blessed Silvester ordered that temple

destroyed and likewise other palaces so that the orators who came to Rome would not wander through profane buildings but instead pass with devotion through the churches. But he had the head and hands of the aforesaid idol laid before his Palace of the Lateran in remembrance of the temple, and they are now falsely called by the vulgar Samson's Ball. And before the Colosseum was a temple where ceremonies were done to the aforesaid image.

VIII

Constantine's Three Great Churches of Rome

During the days of Pope Silvester, Constantine Augustus built the Lateran Basilica, which he adorned beautifully. He put there the Ark of the Covenant, which Titus had carried from Jerusalem with many thousands of Jews, and the Golden Candlestick of Seven Lamps with vessels for oil. In the ark are these things: the golden emeralds, the mice of gold, the Tablets of the Covenant, the Rod of Aaron, manna, the barley loaves, the golden urn, the coat without seam, the reed and garment of Saint John the Baptist, and the tongs that Saint John the Evangelist was shorn with. Moreover he also put in the basilica a ciborium with pillars of porphyry. And he set there four pillars of gilded brass, which the consuls of old had brought to the Capitoline from the Campo Marzio and set in the Temple of Jupiter.

He also made, in the time of the pope and after his prayer, a basilica for the Apostle Peter before Apollo's Temple in the Vatican. The emperor first dug the foundation, and in reverence to the twelve apostles he carried out twelve basketsful of earth. Saint Peter's body is kept as follows. He made a chest closed on all sides with brass and copper, which may not be moved, five feet of length at the head, five at the foot, on the right side five feet and on the left side five feet, five feet above and five feet below. And so he enclosed the body of the Blessed Peter.

He adorned the altar above in the fashion of an arch with bright gold. And he made a ciborium with pillars of porphyry and purest gold. And he set there in front of the altar twelve pillars of glass, which he brought from Greece and which were from Apollo's Temple at Troy. Moreover he set above the Blessed Apostle Peter's body a cross of pure gold weighing one hundred and fifty pounds. On it is written: *Constantinus Augustus et Helena Augusta.*

He also built a basilica for the Blessed Apostle Paul on the Via Ostiense and put his body in brass and copper just like the body of the Blessed Peter.

The same emperor, after he became a Christian and built these churches also gave to the Blessed Silvester a *Phrygium* [Tiara], and white horses, and all the *imperialia* pertaining to the dignity of the Roman Empire. Then he went away to Byzantium. The pope, decorated with these gifts, went forth with Constantine as far as the Roman Arch, where they embraced and kissed each other, and so parted.

PART THREE

A PERAMBULATION OF THE CITY

The Sites of Rome
Region by Region

I

The Vatican and The Needle

Within the Palace of Nero is the Temple of Apollo, which is called Santa Petronilla, before which is the Basilica of the Vatican, adorned with marvelous mosaics and a ceiling of gold and glass. It is called the Vatican because in that place the *Vates, or* priests, sang their offices before Apollo's Temple. All that part of Saint Peter's Church is, therefore, called the Vatican. There is also another temple, which was Nero's wardrobe, which is now called Sant' Andrea. Nearby is the memorial of Caesar, the Needle, where his ashes nobly rest in his sarcophagus, so that, as in his lifetime the whole world lay subdued before him, even in his death the world would lie beneath him forever. The memorial was decorated on the lower part with tablets of gilded brass and with Latin letters beautifully illuminated. And above at the ball, where he rests, it is decorated with gold and precious stones. There it is written:

> Caesar, who once was great as is the world
> Now in how small a cavern art thou closed.

And this memorial was constructed in their style, which is described on it and may still be read. And below in Greek letters these verses are written:

> If one, tell how this stone was set on high;
> If many stones, show where their joints do lie.

II

The Basin and the Golden Pine Cone in Saint Peter's Paradise

In Saint Peter's Paradise is a basin made by Pope Symmachus, constructed with pillars of porphyry that are joined together by marble tablets with griffins and covered with a top of costly brass, with flowers and dolphins of gilt brass pouring forth water. In the middle of the basin is a bronze Pine Cone that, with a roof of gilded brass, covered over the statue of Cybele, mother of the gods, in the opening of the Pantheon. Water out of the Sabbatine Aqueduct was supplied by an underground lead pipe to this Pine Cone. Since it was always full it poured water through the holes in the nuts to all who wanted it. Through the underground pipe some part of the water also flowed to the emperor's bath near the Needle.

III

The Sepulcher of Romulus and the Terebinth of Nero

In the *Naumachia* is the Sepulcher of Romulus, which is called *Meta* or the Goal, which once was encased with marvelous stone. The pavement of the Paradise and the steps of Saint Peter's were made from it. It had an open court around it of twenty feet, paved with stone that came from Tivoli with a drain and a border of flowers. Near it was the Terebinth of Nero. It was no less high than the Castle of Hadrian, which is called Castel Sant' Angelo, encased with marvelous stone. The stonework of the steps and the Paradise was finished from it. This building was round like a castle with two circles with overhanging stones for drainage. Nearby Saint Peter the Apostle was crucified.

IV

Castel Sant' Angelo

There is a castle that was the Temple of Hadrian, as we read in the sermon of the festival of Saint Peter where it says, "The memorial of the Emperor Hadrian, a temple built of marvelous greatness and beauty," which was all covered with stones and adorned with different stories and fenced with bronze railings all around, with golden peacocks and a bull. The two peacocks were those that are in the Basin of the Paradise. At the four sides of the temple were four horses of gilded brass, and on every side were brass gates. In the middle of the circle was a porphyry Sepulcher of Hadrian, which is now in the Lateran before the Fullery and is the Sepulcher of Pope Innocent. The cover is in Saint Peter's Paradise on the prefect's tomb. Below were gates of brass as they now appear. And in the porphyry monument of the Blessed Helen Pope Anastasius IV is buried.

The monuments that we have spoken of were dedicated as temples, and the Roman maidens flocked to them with vows, as Ovid says in the book of *Fasti.*

V

The Mausoleum of Augustus

At the Porta Flaminia Octavian made a castle called Augustum to be the burying place of the emperors. It was encased in different kinds of stone. Inside there is a hollow leading into the circle by hidden passageways. In the lower circle are the sepulchers of emperors and on each sepulcher are inscriptions saying in this manner: "These are the bones and ashes of the Emperor Nerva and such and such was the victory he won." In front of the sepulcher stood the image of the emperor's god, just as with all the other sepulchers. In the middle of the sepulchers is a recess where Octavian used to sit, and the priests there performed their ceremonies. From every kingdom of the world he commanded that one basketful of earth be brought, which he put atop the temple as a reminder to all nations coming to Rome.

VI

Between the Mausoleum of Augustus and the Capitoline

On the top of the Pantheon, that is to say Santa Maria Rotonda, stood the golden Pine Cone that is now in front of the door of Saint Peter's. The church was all covered with tiles of gilded brass, so much so that from afar it seemed to be a mountain of gold. The beauty of this is still discerned in part. And on top of the front of the Pantheon stood two bulls of gilded brass. Before the Palace of Alexander were the two temples of Flora and Phoebus. Behind the palace, where the Shell now is, was the Temple of Bellona. There it was written:

> Old Rome was I, now new Rome shall be praised;
> I bear my head aloft, from ruin raised.

At the Shell of Parione was the Temple of Gnaeus Pompeius, a temple of marvelous greatness and beauty. His monument, called Majorent, was fairly adorned and was an oracle of Apollo. There were other oracles in other places.

The Church of Sant' Urso was Nero's Chancery. In the Palace of Antoninus was the Temple of Divus Antoninus. By San Salvatore, before Santa Maria in

Aquiro, the Temple of Aelian Hadrian and the Arch of Pity. In the Campo Marzio the Temple of Mars, where consuls were elected in the Calends of June and where they stayed until the Calends of January. If the chosen consul was clear of crime his consulship was confirmed here. And because of this custom many are still called Consuls of the Romans. In this temple the Roman conquerors set the rostra of the ships of their enemies, which were made into works to be a sight for all nations. Near the Pantheon was the Temple of Minerva Chalcidica where some pillars of marble are still seen. Behind San Marco the Temple of Apollo. In the Camillanum, where San Cyriaco is, was the Temple of Vesta; in the lime-kiln the Temple of Venus; in the Lady Rose's Monastery the Golden Castle that was the oracle of Juno.

VII

The Capitoline

The capitol is so called because it was the head of the world where the consuls and senators met to govern the world. The face of it was covered with high and strong walls rising above the top of the hill. It was all covered over with glass and gold and marvelous carved work. On the Capitoline were molten images of all the Trojan kings and of the emperors. Within the fortress was a palace completely adorned with marvelous works in gold, silver, brass, and costly stones, to be a mirror to all nations. It was said to be worth one third of the world.

These were the temples that were within the fortress, as far as can be remembered. In the uppermost part of the fortress, over the *Porticus Crinorum,* was the Temple of Jupiter and Moneta, as found in Ovid's martyrology of the *Fasti,* where Jupiter's image of gold sat on a throne of gold. Towards the market-place, the Temple of Vesta and Caesar. There was the chair of the pagan pontiffs, where the senators appointed Julius Caesar in the sixth day of the month of March.

On the other side of the Capitol, over *Cannapara,* the Temple of Juno. Very near the public market-place was the Temple of Hercules. On the Tarpeian Hill was the Temple of Asilis where Julius Caesar was slain by the Senate. In the place where Santa Maria now stands were two temples joined together by a palace. These were the Temple of Phoebus and the Temple of Carmentis where the Emperor Octavian saw the vision in heaven. Close by the Camellaria was the Temple of Janus, who was the warden of the Capitol. It was called the Golden Capitol because it surpassed all the realms of the whole world in wisdom and beauty.

VIII

The Palace and Forum of Trajan

The Palace of Trajan and Hadrian was built nearly all of stones and was adorned throughout with marvelous works. The ceiling was of many different colors. Here is a pillar of marvelous height and beauty, carved with the stories of these emperors like the Pillar of Antoninus at his palace. On the one side was the Temple of Divine Trajan and on the other the Temple of Divine Hadrian.

On the Silversmith's Hill was the Temple of Concord and Saturn. In *Tofula* is the Temple of Bacchus. In the end of the *Insula Argentaria* is the Temple of Vespasian.

On the hill of Santa Maria in Campo is the Temple of Titus. Where San Basilio stands was the Temple of Carmentis. Within these bounds was a palace with two forums, the Forum of Nerva with the Temple of Divine Nerva and the greater Forum of Trajan. In front of the gate was the Temple of the Goddess Juno. Where San Quirico is was the Temple of Jupiter.

In the wall of San Basilio was set in a good and notable place a large tablet of brass where the league between the Romans and Jews in the time of Judas Maccabeus was written.

IX

Near the Mamertine Prison and the Church of San Sergio

In Front of the Mamertine Prison was the Temple of Mars, where his image now is. Near him was the Fatal Temple or Santa Martina. Nearby is the the Temple of Refuge, that is Sant' Adriano. Close by is another Fatal Temple. Near the public prison is the Temple of the Fabii. Behind San Sergio is the Temple of Concord, and before this is the Triumphal Arch. Here was the ascent to the Capitoline by the public Treasury, which was the Temple of Saturn. On the other side was an arch encased in marvelous stones. On it was the story of how the soldiers received their gifts from the Senate through the Treasurer, who had charge of this business. All these gifts he weighed in a balance before they were given to the soldiers. It is called San Salvatore de Statera, which means, of the balance.

X

The Forum

In *Cannapara* is the Temple of Ceres and Tellus with two courts or houses decorated all around with porches resting on pillars so that whoever sat there to give judgment was seen from every side. Near that house was the Palace of Catiline, where there was a Church of Sant' Antonio. Nearby is a place called Hell because in ancient times it burst forth there and brought great mischief upon Rome. Here a certain noble knight, intending that the city should be saved after the gods had given their oracles, put on his harness and cast himself into the pit, and the earth closed. So was the city delivered. There is the Temple of Vesta, which - it is said - a dragon crouches beneath, as we read in the life of Saint Silvester.

The Temple of Pallas is there, and Caesar's Forum, and the Temple of Janus, who views the year with both foresight and hindsight, as Ovid says in the *Fasti.* It is now called Cencio Frangipane's Tower. The Temple of Minerva with an arch is joined to it, but it is now called San Lorenzo in Miranda. Close by is the Church of San Cosma, which was the Temple of Asylum. Behind was the Temple of Peace and Latona, and above it the Temple of Romulus. Behind Santa Maria Nova, double Temple of Concord and Piety. Near the Arch of Seven Lamps, the Temple of Aesculapius, which was called the Cartulary because there was a public library there, of which there were twenty-eight in the city.

XI

The Palatine

Above the Arch of Seven Lamps was the Temple of Pallas and the Temple of Juno. Within the Palatine is the Temple of Julian; in front of the Palatine, the Temple of the Sun; in the Palatine, the Temple of Jupiter, which is called *Casa maior.* At San Caesario was the Auguratory of Caesar. Before the Colosseum was the Temple of the Sun, where there were ceremonies to the image that stood on the top of the Colosseum. On his head he had a crown of gold decorated with gems. The head and hands are now in front of the Lateran. The Septizonium was the Temple of the Sun and Moon. In front of it was the Temple of Fortune. Santa Balbina in *Albiston* was Caesar's Pleasure House. There was a candlestick made of the stone Albiston, which, once kindled and set in the open air, was never, by any means, extinguished. There, moreover, is an image of Our Lord behind the altar, painted by no human hand, portraying Our Lord in the flesh. This place is, therefore, called *Albesta* because the *albae stolae,* that is to say the white stoles of the emperors were made there. There were the Severian and Commodian Baths. At Santa Saba was the Area of Apollo and of Spleen.

XII

The Circus Maximus

The Circus of Priscus Tarquinius was of marvelous beauty. It was built in such a way by degrees that no Roman hindered another from seeing the games. At the top were arches all around, roofed with glass and shining gold. Around it were the houses of the palace above. The women sat here to see the games on the fourteenth day of the Calends of May, when the games were held. In the center were two needles; the smaller was eighty-seven feet high, but the taller was one-hundred twenty-two. On top of the triumphal arch at the head of the circus stood a horseman of gilded brass, which seemed to press forward as though the rider would have the horse run. On another arch at the end stood another horseman of gilded brass in the same pose. These images with all their harnesses of brass were carried away by the emperor Constantine to Constantinople, Damascus and Alexandria. At the level of the palace were chairs for the emperor and the queen, from which they used to watch the games.

XIII

The Caelian Hill to Santa Croce in Gerusalemme

On the Caelian Hill was Scipio's Temple. Before the Maximian Baths were two shells and two temples of Isis and Serapis. In the Orphan House, the Temple of Apollo. In the Palace of the Lateran are things to be marveled at but not to be written. In the Susurrian Palace was the Temple of Hercules.

XIV

The Eastern Quarter of the City

On the Esquiline Hill was the Temple of Marius now called Cimbrum, because he conquered the Cimbrians. Some pillars and images are still visible here. In the Palace of Licinius, the Temple of Honor and Diana. At Santa Maria Maggiore was the Temple of Cybele. At San Pietro in Vincoli was the Temple of Venus. At Santa Maria in Fontana, the Temple of Faunus. Here was the idol that spoke to Julian and beguiled him.

In the Palace of Diocletian were four temples of Aesculapius, Saturn, Mars and Apollo, which are now called the Bushels. At the head of the Three Cross Ways was the Temple of Venus, still called the Garden of Venus. In the Palace of Tiberius, the Temple of the Gods.

On the brow of the hill was the Temple of Jupiter and Diana, that is now called the Emperor's Table, over the Palace of Constantine. There in the palace was the Temple of Saturn and Bacchus, where their idols now lie. Nearby are the Marble Horses. In the Baths of Olympias, where Saint Laurence was broiled, was the Temple of Apollo. Before the Palace of Trajan, where the gate of the palace yet remains, was a temple.

XV

Near The Tiber

On the Aventine was the Temple of Mercury looking toward the Circus and the Temple of Pallas and Mercury's Well, where the merchants received oracles. At the Arch of the Racecourse was the house of Aurelia Auristilla; on one side the Temple of Maecenas and on the other side the Temple of Jupiter.

Near the *Schola Graeca* was the Palace of Lentulus. On the other side where the Tower of Cencius de Orrigo is now was the Temple of Bacchus.

At the gratings was the Temple of the Sun. Santo Stefano Rotondo was the Temple of Faunus. At the Elephant, the Temple of the Sibyl; and the Temple of Cicero at the Tullianum, where now stands the house of Pierleone's sons. There is the *Carcer Tullianus,* or the Tullian Prison, at the Church of San Nicola. Near there is the Temple of Jupiter where the Golden Bower was and the Severian Temple where Sant' Angelo is. At *Velum Aureum,* that is to say the Golden Vail, the Temple of Minerva. At the Jews' Bridge, the Temple of Faunus; at Caccavari, the Temple of Craticula. At the Bridge of Antoninus, the Circus of Antoninus, where Santa Maria in Catarino now is. At Santo Stefano in Piscinula, that is to say, at the Cistern, the Palace of the Prefect Chromatius and a temple called *Holovitreum,* made of glass and gold by mathematical craft. Here was an astrograph with all the signs of the heavens. It was destroyed by Saint Sebastian with Tiburtius, the son of Chromatius.

XVI

Trastevere

In Trastevere, that is, beyond the Tiber, where Santa Maria now is, was the Temple of the Ravennates, where oil flowed from the earth in the time of the Emperor Octavian. There was the Taberna Meritoria, where soldiers, who waited without pay in the Senate, served for wages. Beneath the Janiculum, the Temple of Gorgon. At the river bank where the ships dock, the Temple of Hercules. At the Cistern, the Temple of Fortune and Diana. In the Licaonian Island, the Temple of Jupiter and the Temple of Aesculapius, and the body of the Apostle Saint Bartholomew.

Outside the Appian gate, the Temple of Mars and a triumphal arch.

XVII

Conclusion

These and more temples and palaces of emperors, consuls, senators and prefects were inside this Roman city in the time of the heathen, as we have read in old chronicles, have seen with our own eyes, and have heard the ancient men tell of. In writing we have tried as well as we could to bring back to the human memory how great was their beauty in gold, silver, brass, ivory and precious stones.

GAZETTEER

A

ACQUA SALVIA- – See TRE FONTANE.

ALBISTON – (1.12, 3.11) *Albiston* was a name given to the Church of Santa Balbina in Parco di Porta Capena. The meaning of the name is unknown. Two fanciful derivations are suggested in the text (3.11). The story (1.12, 2.8) refers to the parting of Constantine and Saint Silvester when the emperor was supposed to have surrendered Rome with the supremacy of the Western Empire to the pope, which was an event of great political importance (Donation of Constantine). See Gregorovius 4: 405; Graf 2: 98; Brentano, pp. 84-85.

ALEXANDER'S GOLDEN ARCH – (1.4) The marble arch that was at San Celso under the church tower is said to have fallen down during the time of Pope Urban V (1362-70). (*Anonymus Magliabecchianus,* Urlichs, p. 153.) Jordan (2: 413) identifies this arch with that of Arcadius, Honorius and Theodosius, of which the inscription is preserved in the *Einsiedeln Itinerary.* [II-14]

ALEXANDER'S THEATER – (1.8) The Stadium of Severus Alexander or Piazza Navona. [III-1]

ALEXANDRINE BATHS – (1.6) These were the Baths of Nero, which were extended in the third century by

Alexander Severus from near the Piazza Navona to near the PANTHEON. Also called the Palace of Alexander (3.6). [III-2]

AMPHITHEATER – See COLOSSEUM.

ARCH OF ANTONINUS – (1.4) This was probably the Arch of Claudius, which carried the Acqua Vergine across the Via Flaminia, now the Corso, in front of the Palazzo Sciarra, and which bore an inscription commemorating the emperor's campaign in Britain. The name of Antoninus was borrowed from the neighboring column. [II-1]

ARCH OF THE CIRCUS MAXIMUS – In 1.4 called the Arch of Titus and Vespasian. In 3.12 two are mentioned. See Arch of Titus. Same as Arch of the Racecourse. [II-2]

ARCH OF CONSTANTINE – (1.4) At COLOSSEUM. [II-3]

ARCH OF DRUSUS – (1.4, 1.12) *Intra portam arcus stillae; Arcus stillans ante septemsolium.* The so-called Dripping Arch, at the Porta San Sebastiano, which carried an aqueduct across the Via Appia. The inscription of an arch in the Via Appia in honor of Augustus is preserved in the *Einsiedeln Itinerary.* The description of the arch (1.4) is from the fifteenth century. Saint Stephen, the pope, was imprisoned and held a synod *in carcere ad arcum stellae,* perhaps not the same place. (*Liber Pontificialis* Stephen I). A commentary to Juvenal gives the name *arcus stillaus* to the Porta Capena because the aqueduct went over it. *Schol. ad Juv.* 3.2. [II-4, IV-2]

ARCH OF FAUSTINUS – (1.4) Unidentified.

Arch of the Golden Bread – (1.4) *Arcus panis aurei.* The *Graphia* reads *arcus aureus.* Unidentified. The text locates it on the Capitoline. [II-5]

Arch of Julius Caesar and the Senators – See Arch of Septimius Severus.

Arch of Noah – In referrring to the city founded by Noah (1.1), the writer had probably in mind Arca Noe, the popular name of a monument adjoining the Forum of Nerva. See Nichols, *Mirabiliana,* p. 161; Urlichs, pp. 140, 225. [II.-7]

Arch of Octavian – (1.4) Also Arco di Portogallo. The site of this arch, which crossed the Via Flaminia (Corso), was marked by an inscription on the house, No. 167 Corso, at the corner of the Via della Vite. Its attribution to Octavian is purely arbitrary. It is now generally believed to have been erected in honor of Marcus Aurelius. Some of its sculptures were placed in the Palazzo dei Conservatori. [II-8]

Arch of Piety – (1.4, 3.6) Also Arch of Pity; before Santa Maria in Aquiro. Santa Maria in Aquiro is described in a processional order as being *ad arcum Pietatis.* See Krautheimer, p. 278; also Nichols, *Mirabiliana,* pp. 167-68. De Rossi has conjectured that the widow of the legend (1.4) was, in the original sculpture, a suppliant nation at the feet of the emperor. Lanciani (p. 387) places the Arch of Pity or Piety in an open place opposite the Portico of the Pantheon, possibly confusing the two churches known as Santa Maria Rotonda. [II-9]

Arch of Pity – See Arch of Piety.

ARCH OF SAN MARCO – (I.4) *Arcus manus carneae* is mentioned in a processional order of the twelfth century as lying between SAN MARCO and the HILL OF THE SILVERSMITHS or somewhere in the area of Piazza Venezia. See Nichols, *Mirabiliana,* pp. 169-70. The name *Macel dei Corvi,* still existing in this locality, was thought to be derived from it. This name *(Macellum corvorum)* is given in Bufalini's plan to the Salita di Marsorio. [II-10]

ARCH OF SEPTIMIUS SEVERUS – Also Breeches Towers; and (I.4) Arch of Julius Caesar and the Senators; at the west end of the Roman Forum. It probably gained the name given to it in I.4 from the careless reading of the inscription, still preserved upon it, IMP. CAES.... S.P.Q.R. It was crowned in the Middle Ages by two towers, one of which belonged to the church of Santi Sergio e Bacco. Hence the name, *turres de Bracis.* Nichols, *Rostri,* pp. 63, 65. [II-6]

ARCH OF SEVERUS – The Arch of the Silversmiths at San Giorgio in Velabro is omitted. The *Anonymus* (Urlichs, p. 156.) mentions it at the end of its longer list. The great double Arch of Janus nearby was probably converted into a tower. The Arch of Severus, which is partly under the corner of the campanile, may have been enclosed by other buildings. An inscription preserved in the apse of the church records that in the year 1259 Cardinal Pietro Capocci gave to the church three sites adjoining the campanile, *tres sitas iuxta turrim dicte ecclesie que dicitur ad vallaram, ita quod dicte terre aliquo titulo alienari non possint.* [Three sites near the tower of the said church, which is called in Velabro, so named because they may not be alienated by any title to the said land.] [II-11]

ARCH OF THE SEVEN LAMPS – See ARCH OF TITUS.

ARCH OF THE SILVERSMITHS – See ARCH OF SEVERUS.

ARCH OF TITUS – There were apparently two arches: (1.4, 3.10) The Arch of the Seven Lamps of Titus and Vespasian in the Roman Forum [II-12]; and the Arch of Titus and Vespasian (1.3, 3.12) in the Circus, mentioned in the *Einsiedeln Itinerary,* which records an inscription of an arch *in circo maximo* in honor of Titus.

ARCH OF TITUS AND VESPASIAN – See ARCH OF TITUS.

ARCO DI PORTOGALLO – See ARCH OF OCTAVIAN.

AREA OF APOLLO AND SPLEEN – (3.11) *Area Apollinis et Splenis.* From the *Notitia,* Region 1, *Porta Capena.* The locality is probably arbitrary.

AUGURATORY OF CAESAR – Located in 3.11 on the PALATINE. The *Auguratorium* (not *Caesaris*) occurs in the *Notitia,* Region 10, *Palatium.* The Auguratorium on the Palatine is east of the TEMPLE OF CYBELE. It is identified as the place where Romulus took auspices for the founding of Rome (*Blue Guide,* p. 123).

AVENTINE – The southernmost of the Seven Hills, southeast of the CIRCUS MAXIMUS. [I-III]

B

BASILICA JULIA – See CANNAPARA.

BASILICA OF JUPITER – See TEMPLE OF JUPITER.

BASILICA SESSORIANA – See SANTA CROCE IN GERUSALEMME.

BATHS OF AGRIPPA – (1.6) Formerly connected with the PANTHEON. [III-3]

BATHS OF ANTONINUS – See BATHS OF CARACALLA.

BATHS OF CARACALLA – (1.6) The Baths of Antoninus; just south of the Caelian Hill between Porta Capena and Porta Ardeatina. [III-4]

BATHS OF CONSTANTINE – See the PALACE OF CONSTANTINE.

BATHS OF THE CORNUTI – (2.12) Unidentified.

BATHS OF DIOCLETIAN – (1.6) At Piazza della Republica. [III-6]

BATHS OF DOMITIAN – (1.6) The Baths of Trajan, northeast of the COLOSSEUM. [III-7]

BATHS OF LICINIUS – Unidentified; see Licinian Palace.

BATHS OF NERO – See ALEXANDRINE BATHS.

BATHS OF OLYMPIAS – Unidentified; 1.12 claims this as the place of Saint Laurence's martyrdom in Panisperna, but it is not named in the Acts of Saint Laurence. The Baths of Sallust appear to be the place of his martyrdom. (*Acta S. Laurentii,* 10 Aug., 519). [IV-17]

BATHS OF TIBERIUS – (1.6) Perhaps the name of other ruins, not public baths. The *Anonymus* claims that they are behind SANTA SUSANNA, broken down by age, probably in the Garden of Sallust. There are also the so-called Baths of Tiberius below the Palace of Domitian on the PALATINE.

BREECHES TOWERS – See ARCH OF SEPTIMIUS SEVERUS.

BRIDGE OF ANTONINUS – (1.9) *Pons Antoninus,* the *Pons Aurelius* of the *Notitia,* the modern Ponte Sisto in the region called Arenula; broken down before 1018, rebuilt 1475. [I-II]

BRIDGE OF THEODOSIUS – See VALENTINIAN BRIDGE.

THE BUSHELS – (3.14) *Nunc vocantur modii.* The round form of parts of the ruin of the BATHS OF DIOCLETIAN no doubt suggested this name. One of the Bushels is now the Church of San Bernardo alle Terme. [III-9]

C

CAESAREAN PALACE – See GREATER PALACE.

CAESAR'S NEEDLE -See SAINT PETER'S NEEDLE.

CAESAR'S PLEASURE HOUSE – (3.11) *Mutatorium Caesaris.* From the *Notitia,* Region 1, *Porta Capena.* The locality is probably arbitrary.

CAMELLARIA – See TEMPLE OF CARMENTIS.

CAMILLANUM – See PALACE OF CAMILLUS.

CAMPO MARZIO – (3.6) In the twelfth century a restricted space, possibly at the piazza now so named, where some ancient remains are embedded into the walls of the buildings.

CANNAPARA – (1.12, 3.7, 3.10) This appears to have been in the ruins of the Basilica Julia in the ROMAN FORUM. It is identified with the locality *in Tellure* or *locus Telluris* (also *in Tellude* and *Telludis Templum*), which occur frequently in the Acts of the Saints and elsewhere as the place where the *Praefectus Urbis* held his tribunal, whereas the ancient Temple of Tellus was in the quarter called Carinae near the Subura. The basilica, which was principally used as a law court, was erroneously identified with the Temple of Tellus, attributed by ecclesiastical tradition to the same use. The remains of the Basilica Julia were in a garden belonging to the hospital of Our Lady of Consolation and were used for a long period of time as a quarry, as is evidenced by the leases or licenses granted for that purpose, preserved among the records of the hospital. [IV-12]

CAPITOLINE – Also the Tarpeian Hill. The smallest but most famous of the Seven Hills. It is quite uncertain whether any special part of the Capitoline was known as the Tarpeian Hill in Mirabilian times. The northeastern end of the Capitoline was occupied in the twelfth century by the *Tabularium,* restored about 1143 as the Senators' Palace or the SENATE and by the Abbey of SANTA MARIA IN ARACOELI, to which in the beginning of the century the whole hill "with its stones, walls and columns" belonged. See Bull of Anacletus II, Nichols, *Mirabiliana,* pp.176-79. The remainder of the hill appears to have become a rough garden or pasture studded with ruins provided with imaginary names. Such was the power of its old associations, however, that the Capitoline was regarded as one of the "Seven Wonders of the World." During the three following centuries the ruins were doubtless used to supply materials for the new construction of the palace and the monastery. Poggio gives a description of the desolate condition of the hill about 1450. He describes himself as sitting in the ruins of the Tarpeian fortress behind what seemed the huge threshold of the door of a temple with broken columns about, the spot being one that commanded a view of the greatest part of the city. It is probably these ruins that are shown in the plan copied at the end of the Nichols volume. Poggio Bracciolini, *Historia de fortunae varietate,* 1: 5, in Urlichs, p. 235.

The *Porticus Crinorum,* or part of it, was between SAN NICOLA IN CARCERE and the Capitol (Nichols, *Mirabiliana,* p. 158). High above on this side of the hill appear to have been the remains of the fourth corner of the Capitoline Temple of Jupiter (*Templum maius quod respicit super Alaphantum;* Bull of Anaclete II, Nichols, *Mirabiliana,* p. 176-79).

The opening of the description of the CAPITOLINE (3.7) appears to be a reminiscense of the statues of the kings mentioned by Appian, *Bellum Civicum,* 1.16; Dio, 43.45; Pliny 24.5, 11; Suetonius, *Julius* 76.

CARTULARY TOWER – (1.4, 3.11) The Cartulary Tower, near the ARCH OF TITUS, was a papal archive in connection with a palace existing on this side of the Palatine in the eighth and ninth centuries. De Rossi, *Bulletino del Istituto,* 1884, p. 5. It was afterwards part of the Frangipane fortress and was destroyed in 1237. [V-1]

CASA MAIOR – See GREATER PALACE.

CASTEL SANT' ANGELO – (1.8, 3.3) The Mausoleum of Hadrian, Hadrian's Castle or the Castle of Crescentius. In the tenth century popularly called *domus Theodorici,* obtained the name Castle of Crescentius after its obstinate defense by Crescentius against the Emperor Otto III in 998. Before the end of the twelfth century it was called

Castel Sant' Angelo. Gregorovius 3: 520, 4: 343. The sermon mentioned (3.4) by an unknown author follows the sermons of Leo the Great in manuscripts of that work. It contains nothing further about the monument named here. *Leonis Magni Opera,* Venice. 1753. *Appendix Sermonum,* n. xvi, f. 442. The two bronze peacocks mentioned (3.4) are now in the Giardino della Pigna at the Vatican.

CASTLE OF CRESCENTIUS – See CASTEL SANT' ANGELO.

CATACOMB – See CEMETERY.

CEMETERY OF *AGER VERANUS* – (I.II) At SAN LORENZO FUORI LE MURA, perhaps the Catacombs of Santa Cyriaca, near the Campo Verano. [IV-I]

CEMETERY OF BALBINA – (I.II) On the Via Ardeatina. [IV-II]

CEMETERY BETWEEN TWO BAYS – (I.II) *Inter duos lauros.* The burial place of Saint Helena on the Via Labicana.

CEMETERY OF CALEPODIUS – (I.II) At Porta San Pancrazio on the Gianicolo. [IV-III]

CEMETERY OF CALLISTO – (I.II) Apparently two are mentioned by this name: one on the Via Appia near SANTI FABIANO E SEBASTIANO [IV-IV]; and an unidentified catacomb near the PORTA SALARIA.

CEMETERY OF THE CAPPED BEAR – See CEMETERY OF URSO.

CEMETERY AT THE CUCUMBER HILL – (I.II) *Cimiterium clivi cucumeris.* The oldest copies of the *Mirabilia* have *cimiterium cucumeris.* The spot, locus qui dicitur cucumeris, is described by William of Malmesbury (pp. 368-69) as near the point where the Via Pinciana joined the Via Salaria. [IV-V]

CEMETERY OF THE INNOCENTS – (I.II) At San Paolo; unidentified, possibly at Tre Fontane.

CEMETERY OF PRAETEXTATUS – (I.II) Near the beginning of the Via Appia Pignatelli. [IV-VI]

CEMETERY OF PRISCILLA – (I.II) On Via Salaria near the Piazza di Priscilla. [IV-VII]

CEMETERY OF SANT' AGATA – (I.II) This cemetery was near the Porta San Pancrazio (PORTA AURELIA). The *girolus* was the CIRCUS OF CALIGULA. The name "Agata" may have been suggested by Agapita, the name of a saint buried there. [IV-VIII]

CEMETERY OF SANT' AGNESE – (I.II) At the Church of Sant' Agnese fuori le Mura, north of the city outside the Porta Pia. [IV-IX]

CEMETERY OF SAN CYRIACO – (I.II) Unidentified; on the Via Ostiense.

CEMETERY OF SANTI ERMIO AND DOMITILLA – (I.II) Catacombs of Santa Domitilla on Via delle Sette Chiese, south of the Via Appia. The Catacomb of Nereo and Achilleo is known as the Catacomb of Domitilla. [IV-XI]

CEMETERY OF SAN FELICE – (I.II) Unidentified.

CEMETERY OF SANTA FELICITA – (I.II) North of the Villa Torlonia on Via Simeto. [IV-X]

CEMETERY OF SAN MARCELLO – (1.11) On the old Via Salaria; unidentified.

CEMETERY OF SAINT PETER'S WELL – (1.11) *Cimiterium fontis* [or *ad nympham*] *sancti Petri.* The *fons S. Petri* was on Via Nomentana, where Peter was said to have baptized. De Rossi, *Roma Sotterranea* 1: 159, 179. [IV-XII]

CEMETERY OF TRASO – (1.11) At San Saturnino; near the Villa Ada at Via Tara and Via Salaria. [IV-XIII]

CEMETERY OF URSO – (1.11) There has been a transposition of names. It should be the CEMETERY OF THE CAPPED BEAR *(ursi pileati)* in the Via Portuensis and the CEMETERY OF URSO at SANTA VIVIANA within the walls. De Rossi, *Roma Sotterranea* 1: 175-83. [IV-XIV]

CIMBRUM – The images, mentioned in 3.14, commonly called the Trophies of Marius, were removed in 1585 to the balustrade of the Piazza del Campidoglio.

CIRCUS OF ANTONINUS – (3.15) *Circus* [or *arcus*] *Antonini.* The THEATER OF ANTONINUS by the BRIDGE OF ANTONINUS is listed in section 1.8. The same monument is, no doubt, meant in both places, probably the Theater of Balbus. However, Santa Maria in Catarino [or *Cataneo*], the same as Santa Caterina de Rota, is not in this vicinity. Martinelli, *Roma Sacra,* p. 371. [III-10]

CIRCUS OF CALIGULA – (1.12) The ruins of the Circus of Caligula at the Vatican were called the PALACE OF NERO (3.1) and the Palace of Caligula. Near this, according to church tradition, was a TEMPLE OF APOLLO. *Sepultus est* (Sanctus Petrus) *via Aurelia in templo Apollinis iuxta locum ubi crucifixus est, iuxta palatium Neronianum in Vaticano, iuxta territorium Triumphale, in Calendas Julias.* Anastasius, *Liber Pontificialis.* [III-11]

Circus Flaminius – (1.8) Probably between the Tiber and the Portico of Octavia (*Blue Guide,* p. 80). The text of the *Mirabilia* appears to confuse it with the Theater of Marcellus [I-3, III-16]. The Flaminian Theater may be the Circus Flaminius, but if this interpretation is correct, not only the Colosseum, which might seem to form a class by itself, but the Theater of Marcellus is omitted from this chapter. Perhaps the latter building is denoted by the term *Theatrum Flaminium.* When the remains of the Flaminian Circus had become obscure, the name may have been transferred to the more conspicious ruin, which seems to have been included in the stronghold of Pierleone. The Circus Flaminius referred to (1.12 from *Acta S. Marcelli,* 16 Jan. 371) as at the Jews' Bridge was also perhaps the Theater of Marcellus. See the end of 1.12 and also Nichols, *Mirabiliana,* p. 158. In the medieval Acts of Saint Agnes the prefect comes *ad theatrum,* that is to say, to the Alexandrine Stadium. Mombritius, f. 18. The *castellum aureum* was the Circus Flaminius. Martinelli, p. 87.

Circus of Hadrian – (1.8) Near Castel Sant' Angelo; called Nero's Theater. [III-12]

Circus Maximus – Introduced (1.8) not by its popular name of Stadium, but learnedly as the Theater of Tarquin and the Emperors and (3.12) as the Circus of Priscus Tarquinius (Livy 1.35). The form of the seats alluded to (3.12) is shown in the drawings of the sixteenth century. The descriptions *(in alio arcu qui est in fine)* seem to imply that two arches were standing in the twelfth century. Only one is mentioned in 1.4 *(in circo arcus Titi et Vespasiani),* unless *arcus* is here treated as plural. See Arch of Titus. The arch at the round end belonged in the tenth century to the monastery of San Gregorio and was transferred in 1145 to the Frangipane. Mittarelli,

Annales Cameracenses, 1 App. 96, 3 App. 417, cited by Jordan 2: 514. Constantine added to the ornament of the circus, and his son Constantius erected the greater obelisk. The text (3.12) is founded on a mistaken reminiscence of the plunder of Roman monuments by Constans II in 663, when the bronze roof of the PANTHEON was removed. [III-13]

Duae aguliae: two obelisks, the greater of which, somewhat shortened at the base, is now at the Lateran and the lesser in the Piazza del Popolo. The heights are from the Region Book. Urlichs, p. 21.

CIRCUS OF PRISCUS TARQUINIUS – See CIRCUS MAXIMUS.

THE CISTERN – (3.15, 3.16) *In piscina.* There is a little church between the island and Santa Cecilia called San Benedetto in Piscinula (*in Piscina,* Cencius in Mabillon, *Museum Italicum,* 2: 193), where Saint Benedict is said to have lived (Martinelli, p. 79).

CLIVUS ARGENTARIUS – See HILL OF THE SILVERSMITHS.

COLOSSEUM – (1.7, 1.12, 2.5, 2.7, 3.11) *Colosseum Amphitheatrum (Colossus amphitheatri, Graphia).* The *Notitia,* in the fourth region, mentions *Colossum altum pedes centrum duo semis,* which the text presents as one hundred and eight submissal feet. The actual height should be about one hundred eighty-seven feet measured on the outside. No meaning has been suggested for the word *submissales.* It seems to have arisen out of the *semis* of the *Notitia.* After the removal of the statue (described below), the name of Colossus passed to the Amphitheater. The amphitheater was begun by Vespasian between 70 and 76 AD. In some of the early plans published by De

Rossi *(Piante)* the Colosseum is represented with a dome according to the description in 2.7.

Chapter 2.7 is found in fourteenth century manuscripts. Higden (1: 234) gives the following account of the Colossus, which he assumes was brought from Rhodes:

> This brazen statue, gilded with imperial gold, continually shed rays through the darkness and turned round in even movement with the sun, carrying his face always opposite to the solar body; and all the Romans, when they came near, worshipped in token of subjection. The which Saint Gregory destroyed by fire, as he might not do so by strength; and only the head and the right hand holding a sphere outlasted the fire, and they are now upon two marble pillars before the palace of my lord Pope. And it is a marvel how the founder's craft hath so informed the stubborn brass, that the hair seemeth soft to the sight and the mouth as though it were speaking.

A colossal head and hand are represented as lying before the LATERAN PALACE in a plan of the thirteenth or fourteenth century published by De Rossi, *Piante,* tav. 1. Benjamin of Tudela speaks of the Samson before the Lateran as if it were an entire statue. The bronze head formerly at the Lateran is believed now to be in the court of the Palazzo dei Conservatori. The statue, now associated with Constantine, is actually believed to have been the Colossus of Nero from the vestibule of the Domus Aurea across the way. This statue was 99 feet high in gilt bronze. The companion statue Sol was evidently never completed.

The text of 2.7 transfers the Colossus from the outside to the interior of the Amphitheater, which is itself converted into a temple. In the ecclesiastical tradition it retained its true place. According to the legend, Abdon and Sennen were taken to the Colosseum, before the image of the Sun, and commanded to make sacrifice to the idol (see 2.5). So in the earlier *Mirabilia,* the Sun Temple is before the Colosseum (see 3.11). This is remembered at the end of 2.7. [III-14]

COLUMN OF ANTONINUS – (1.7, 1.10, 3.8) Also Pillar of Antoninus; discovered near Piazza Montecitorio; confused in the sixteenth century with the Column of Marcus Aurelius. See Mason, p. 92. *Columpna Antonini coclidis* (1.10); *Columna Antonini in palaitio suo* (3.8). [I-7]

COLUMN OF TRAJAN – (1.7, 1.10, 3.8) Also Pillar of Trajan. In the FORUM OF TRAJAN before the TEMPLE OF TRAJAN. [I-6]

CONSTANTINE'S HORSE – (2.3) There seems to be some reason for thinking that the bronze statue of Marcus Aurelius, which was before the LATERAN PALACE as early as the tenth century and was known as the Horse of Constantine, was the statue that had been called by the same name in the Forum, and which appears to have been there still in the ninth century. (*Einsiedeln Itinerary,* Urlichs, p. 71). De Rossi suggests that in the decay of arts, as evidenced by the use of the Trajan sculptures in the ARCH OF CONSTANTINE, a statue of Marcus Aurelius may have been dedicated by the Senate to Constantine. There is no actual proof of identity beyond the disappearance of the name in one place and its appearance in the other. The statue at the Lateran, according to Higden (*Polychronicon* I: 228) was called Theodoric by the pilgrims, Constantine by the people, and Marcus or Quintus Curtius by the clergy. He tells a story similar to that given in the text of a knight called Marcus.

Montfaucon (p. 301) concluded from the description of the statue at the end of 2.3 that there was formerly the figure of a captive under the statue. This conjecture appears to find some confirmation in another legendary explanation of the work, according to which it represented Constantine trampling under his horse's feet a dwarf whom his wife received as a lover (Graf 2: 110). The bird is represented by a tuft of hair between the horses ears.

D

DIOSCURI – (2.2) The statues on the Quirinal of Castor and Pollux. The legend of Phidias and Praxiteles and that of the Bronze Horse in 2.3 are evidently stories that had their own origin on the spot out of the fancy of pilgrims or their guides.

Nothing further is known of the sitting statue of the female, which appears from this passage to have been on the Quirinal in front of the Marble Horses. Nichols suggested that possibly some of its remains may be found in the colossal sitting figure Hygieia in the Palazzo Giustiniani, remarkable for the large folds of the serpent surrounding the figure. These folds, without their restored head, might be taken for several serpents. Of the present figure the knees and part of the serpent are original, perhaps not much else. See Matz *Antik Bildwerke in Rom* 1: 227; *Galleria Giustiniani,* plate 8; Clarac, *Musée de Sculpture,* no. 890.

The words added to imply that the statue of the woman signifies the Church encompassed by rolls of scripture are found only in the edition of Montfaucon. The earlier manuscripts are imperfect here and have only the words *praedicatores qui praedicaverunt eam.*

DOMINE QUO VADIS – (1.3) On the Via Appia just before the fork. According to tradition, Christ appeared here to Saint Peter, who was fleeing persecution and martyrdom in Rome. Peter asked Christ, "Where are you going?" and Jesus replied, "I go to Rome to be crucified anew." Peter returned to Rome and his death. The footprints in this church are a reproduction. The originals are in the pilgrimage church of San Sebastiano on Via Appia in the apsidal chapel on the right. The vessel referred to (1.3) is in the octagonal chapel of San Giovanni in Oleo. Actually this chapel marks the spot where traditionally the saint emerged unharmed from a cauldron of boiling oil. [IV-1]

DRIPPING ARCH – See ARCH OF DRUSUS.

E

THE ELEPHANT – (3.15) *In Alephanto.* Probably the *elefantus herbarius* of Region 8 (*Notitia,* Urlichs, p. 12). Elephantus also occurs in the *Einsiedeln Itinerary,* apparently between the Theater of Marcellus and the *SCHOLA GRAECA,* i.e. Santa Maria in Cosmedin (Urlichs, p. 68; Jordan 2: 657). In a redrawing of the Strozzi map (original ca. 1450), reproduced here from the Nichols edition, the name *templum Sibyllae* is given to that church.

EMPEROR'S TABLE – (3.14) Referred to as Temple of Jupiter and Diana; near the Baths of Constantine on the Quirinal. The ruin called *mensa imperatoris,* and later Frontispizio di Nerone, is known by many drawings and engravings. It appears to have been partly destroyed at the end of the seventeenth century and partly in 1722.

ESQUILINE – (1.5) The highest, most extensive and easternmost of the hills on the right side of the Tiber. The singular name alluded to, *Exquilinus qui supra* [or *super*] *alios dicitur,* is mentioned in Peter de Natalibus: *Hic edificavit ecclesiam Sanctae Dei Genitricis, quae dicitur ad Praesepe et hodie Major vocatur, in monte Superagio iuxta macellum Libyae. Acta S. Sixti III.* See also Adinolfi, *Roma* 2: 147.

F

FABRICIAN BRIDGE – (1.9, 3.15) Also Jews' Bridge, from Lungotevere to Tiber Island near Theater of Marcellus.

FASCIOLA – (1.12) Named for the bandage that fell from the wounds of Saint Peter when he was fleeing the MAMERTINE PRISON. At the Church of SANTI NEREO ED ACHILLEO, between the Baths of Caracalla and the Church of SAN SISTO.

FATAL TEMPLE – (1.4, 3.9) At the northwest end of the ROMAN FORUM. This name was suggested by the name, *in Tribus Fatis,* given to the site of the Church of SANTE LUCA E MARTINA, probably by the Sibyl's statues, called the Three Fates. (Procopius, *Bellum Gothorum,* 1.25; *Liber Pontificialis* Leo III, sect. 413.) If there is no misreading, the second Fatal Temple may have been the ruin described by Labacco and others and thought by some archeologists to be the Janus of Domitian and by others to be part of the Aemilian Basilica. Labacco, *Architettura,* tav. 17; Lanciani, *Atti dei Lincei,* ser. 3, II: l; Hülsen, *Annali dell' Istituto,* 1884, p. 323. [V-17]

FLAMINIAN THEATER – See CIRCUS FLAMINIUS.

FORUM – (3.7) In partem fori. The ancient ROMAN FORUM seems to be out of the question, as it had ceased to be a public place, and there is no sign of its location being remembered Jordan (2: 462) suggests the Piazza del Campidoglio as a fit place for the enthronement of Caesar. The Piazza d'Aracoeli was a marketplace in the twelfth century. See Bull of Anacletus II in Nichols, *Mirabiliana,* p. 177. [1-2]

FORUM OF CAESAR – (3.10) The Mirabilian Forum of Caesar lay to the right of the road leading from Sant' Adriano to the TEMPLE OF MINERVA in the FORUM OF NERVA. Nichols, *Mirabiliana,* pp. 166-67. [1-2]

FORUM OF NERVA – (3.8) One of the Imperial Fora; also known as the *Forum Transitorium.* [1-2]

FORUM OF PEACE AND LATONA – See TEMPLE OF PECAE AND LATONA.

FORUM OF TRAJAN – (3.8) One of the Imperial Fora. The gate of the Forum of Trajan may have been the Porta dei Pantani, which appears to have been closed. See Nichols, *Mirabiliana,* pp. 161, 167, 170. [1-2]

FOUR PILLARS OF GILDED BRASS – (2.8) The bronze columns are believed, according to Nichols, to be those that are now at the altar of the Sacrament in the Lateran, and in the table preserved in the cloister by the sacristy. They are said to have been brought from Jerusalem by Titus. Urlichs cites the following extract from the Cod. Vat. Lat. 1984, *ad hist. misc.,* f. 54, *in margine*: "Augustus, conqueror of all Egypt, took from the sea fight many *rostra* or ship-beaks, therewith he made four molten pillars that were afterward set by Domitian on the Capitoline; and which we see to this day, as they were at a later time well ordered by the Emperor Constantine the Great in the Basilica of Saint Savior." Urlichs, p. 117.

FRANGIPANE'S TOWER – (3.10) Cencio Frangipane was a leader of one of the Roman factions in the first half of the twelfth century. The fortresses of this family, which included the ARCH OF TITUS, appear also to have extended across the bottom of the Sacra Via. The tower, built on a ruin called the TEMPLE OF JANUS here, may have rested on a part of the BASILICA JULIA. It is united with an ancient arch to the Church of SAN LORENZO IN MIRANDA, that is, to the Temple of Faustina. A massive arch of masonry, which existed until the middle of the sixteenth century near the west corner of this temple and is shown in several early drawings, has been conjectured to be the arch mentioned here and possibly the remains of the Arch of Fabius. See the *Proceedings of the Roman Archeological Institute,* 1888. [V-2]

FRONTISPIZIO DI NERONE – See EMPEROR'S TABLE.

FULLERY – (3.4) *Ante folloniam.* The sepulcher referred to in the text belonged to Pope Innocent II who died 24 September 1143. Johannes Diaconus, who wrote under Alexander V (1254-61) places his borrowed sarcophagus in the nave of the church. Mabillon, *Museum Italicum* 2: 568. See Nichols, *Mirabiliana,* p. 163.

G

GARDEN OF LUCINA – See SAN PAOLO FUORI LE MURA.

GARDEN OF VENUS – (3.14) *Hortus Veneris* occurs in a papal bull, attributed to John III but probably of the twelfth century, relating to the boundaries of the parish of Santi Apostoli. Jordan 2: 526, 669; Urlichs, p. 200.

GATES – (1.3) Named in the order of their position beginning with the Porta San Paolo and ending with the Porta Flaminia, or the modern Porta del Popolo, and the gate that closed the Ponte Sant' Angelo.

GOLDEN BOWER – See GOLDEN VAIL.

GOLDEN CASTLE – See CIRCUS FLAMINIUS.

GOLDEN VAIL – (1.12) *Est ibi velum aureum*; (3.15) *Ad velum aureum*. The medieval corruption of the ancient Velabrum; another corrupted form occurs in an inscription. See ARCH OF SEVERUS.

GORDIAN'S CEMETERY – (1.11) Outside the PORTA LATINA.

GRADUS ELIOGABALI – (1.12) Steps of Eliogabalus; apparently on the PALATINE HILL near the GREATER PALACE. (*Acta S. Sebastiani*, 20 Jan. 642). [IV-10]

GRATIAN'S BRIDGE – (1.9) Ponte Cestio, between the Island and Trastevere. [I-14]

THE GRATINGS – (3.15) *Ad gradellas*. Jordan (2: 531, 534) suggested that the Church of Santa Maria Egiziaca was the same as Santa Maria de Gradellis (Cencius in Mabillon, *Museum Italicum*, 2: 192). Krautheimer (p. 167) confirms this and identifies the church as the Temple of Fortuna Virilis at Piazza Bocca di Verità. The fluted half-columns may have suggested the name, but there was also a Church of San Gregorio de Gradellis. See Urlichs, p. 173.

GREATER PALACE – (1.7, 3.11) *Casa Maior* or Caesarian Palace. This is the imperial palace complex on the

Palatine. The remains were called palatium maius throughout the Middle Ages. [V-3]

H

HADRIAN'S BRIDGE – See PONTE SANT' ANGELO.

HELL – (3.10) *Locus qui dicitur infernus, eo quod antiquo tempore ibi eructuabat.* This name is still preserved in the Church of Santa Maria Libera nos a Poenis Inferni. The hollow vaults under the towering ruins of the PALATINE seem to have suggested fearful associations, which recalled at the same time the yawning pit of Curtius and the legendary cave of Saint Silvester.

HILL OF SCAURUS – (1.12) *Clivus Scauri, qui est inter amphitheatrum et stadium,* was the residence of Saint Gregory the Great (590-604), where the Church of San Gregorio Magno now stands. Rebuilt, perhaps by Gregory II (715-31); completely rebuilt in the seventeenth and eighteenth centuries. Near this was the SEPTIZONIUM or Seven Floors – *Septizonium Severi,* in Mirabilian nomenclature called *septemsolium* or *septem solia.*

HILL OF THE SILVERSMITHS – (3.8) *Clivus Argentarius*; a hill descending into the ROMAN FORUM passing the MARMERTINE PRISON.

HUT OF FAUSTULUS – (1.7) On the PALATINE; unidentified.

I

IMPERIAL PALACES OF THE PALATINE – See GREATER PALACE.

INTERLUDE – (1.12) *Interlude, id est inter duos ludos.* A few lines below we find: *in Tellure, id est in Cannapara.* See also 3.10. The locality called *in Tellure,* or *locus Telluris* (also *in Tellude* and *Telludis templum*), occurs frequently in the Acts of the Saints and elsewhere as the place where the *praefectus urbis* held his tribunal. *Liber Pontificialis,* Cornelius 5; *Acta S. Gordiani,* 10 May 551: *S. Crescentiani,* 16 Jan. 370, 372; *S. Marii,* 19 Jan. 580; *S. Stephani,* 2 Aug. 142; *S. Sixti,* 6 Aug. 141; *S. Abundii,* 16 Sept. 301. The Temple of Tellus was near the Subura, *in Carinis.* See *Corpus Inscriptionum Latinorum,* 1: 145. See CANNAPARA. [IV-7]

J

JEWS' BRIDGE – See FABRICIAN BRIDGE.

JULIUS CAESAR'S PALACE – (1.7) On the PALATINE; no doubt confused with the GREATER PALACE.

L

Lady Rose's Monastery – (3.6) The *monasterium dominae Rosae* is now Santa Caterina dei Funari opposite Palazzo Mattei in the Ghetto. Martinelli, p. 87.

Lateran Gate – (1.3) The Porta San Giovanni and the ancient Porta Asinaria at San Giovanni in Laterano.

Lateran Palace – (1.7) The name "Lateran" actually comes from the family of Plautius Lateranus, who was deprived of his property and put to death by Nero. See Hibbert, p. 329. [v-5]

Leonine City – (1.2) Vatican City.

Libraries – (3.10) The number of libraries is taken from the *Notitia.* Urlichs, p. 21.

Licaonian Island – (3.6) The Tiber Island. The name, *insula Lycaonia,* occurs in some of the *Acta Martyrum.* The temples of Jupiter and Aesculapius are associated by Ovid (*Fasti* 1.291):

Accepit Phoebo nymphaque Coronide natum
Insula, dividua quam premit amnis aqua.
Iupiter in parte est; cepit locus unus utrumque,
Iunctaque sunt magno templa nepotis avo.

Licinian Palace – Appears to have been in the Region called the *Caput Tauri* in the Middle Ages, near the Porta San Lorenzo. The Temple of Honor and Diana is thought to be suggested by some knowledge of an *aedes Honoris et Virtutis,* founded by Caius Marius. Vitruvius, Book 7, Preface. Cicero *Pro Sestio,* 54, 56; *Corpus Inscriptionum Latinorum* 1: 290. Jordan 2: 319, 518. [v-4]

LIME-KILN – (3.6) *In Calcarari.* In the twelfth century San Nicola ai Cesarini was called San Nicola Calcariorum (*Ordo Censii* in Mabillon, *Museum Italicum,* 2: 194). This church, on the site of Largo Argentina, was demolished in 1932. Lucius Faunus calls it San Nicola in Calcaria (*Roma Ant.*, f. 143). The ruins behind this church, now called the Temple of Hercules Custos, may be the Mirabilian TEMPLE OF VENUS of 3.6.

M

MAJORENT – (3.6) *Maioretum* or *Miorentum*; this was perhaps part of the buildings grouped with the THEATER OF POMPEY. A church of Santa Maria in Majurente occurs in the twelfth century. Cencius in Mabillon, *Museum Italicum* 2: 195.

MAMERTINE PRISON – (1.12) *Privata Mamertini.* The ancient *Carcer* and the traditional prison of the Apostles Peter and Paul outside the northwest corner of the ROMAN FORUM. Opposite it was the statue of a river-god, miscalled Mars, more lately Marsorio. *Privata Mamertini* occurs in the *Acta S. Stephani Papae.* Mombritius 2: 274. [IV-13]

MARKET PLACE – (3.7) It is not clear whether the *forum* mentioned is the same as the *forum publicum* named later in the text. Bunsen (3, 2: 128) suggests the Piazza del Campidoglio.

MAUSOLEUM OF AUGUSTUS – (3.5) The Mausoleum or Sepulcher of Augustus, east of the river above the Ponte Cavour, seems never to have lost the name of its great founder. The name *Augustum* is found in the eighth century and continued to the twelfth. It was known in the tenth century as *Mons Augustus.* Its name was corrupted in Italian to *Austa* or *L'austa.* In the thirteenth it was called *Augusta,* and in the fifteenth it was popularly known as *L'austa.* Gregorovius 3: 550-51, 4: 252; *Anonymus Magliabecchianus,* Ulrichs, p. 162. The emperor Nerva was, in fact, buried in the Mausoleum of Augustus. Jordan suspected that the writer had some knowledge of a base inscribed with his name, which may have been dug out of the monument at the time. The now well-known inscriptions:

> OSSA AGRIPPINAE M. AGRIPPAE, OSSA C. CAESARIS AUGUSTI F. PRINCIPIS INVENTUTIS

etc., derived from the same source, were not known to the earlier epigraphists (Jordan 2: 435). The base inscribed to Agrippina was moved to the court of the Palazzo dei Conservatori. [1-8]

MAXIMIAN BATHS – (1.6, 3.13) The Maximian Baths occur in the list of baths (1.6) but nothing is known about them.

MAUSOLEUM OF HADRIAN – See CASTEL SANT' ANGELO.

MERCURY'S WELL – See TEMPLE OF MERCURY.

MILVIAN BRIDGE – See PONTE MILVIO.

N

NAUMACHIA – (3.3) The name *Naumachia* in the region of the Vatican first appears in the life of Leo III (796-816), who founded a hospital *in loco qui Naumachia dicitur (Liber Pontificialis).* The hospital was dedicated to Saint Peregrinus, and its site is marked by the little Church of San Pellegrino near the Porta Angelica. But the name extended over a wide area. A *regio Naumachiae* appears in the Acts of Saint Sebastian, and the LEONINE CITY was popularly said to be in *Almachia (Anonymus Magliabecchianus,* Ulrichs, pp. 149, 161). Possibly the site where the name first appears by San Pellegrino may indicate the position of one of the naval amphitheaters of imperial times. See Krautheimer, p. 13.

NERONIAN BRIDGE – (1.9) Built near the present Ponte Vittorio Emmanuele by Nero; later called *Triumphalis* and *Vaticanus* (Hibbert, p. 332).

NERO'S CHANCERY – (3.6) *Secretarium Neronis.* The Church of SANT' URSO referred to may be the one near the PONTE SANT' ANGELO.

NERO'S PALACE – (1.7) The LATERAN PALACE; see also the CIRCUS OF CALIGULA. [V-5]

NERO'S THEATER – See CIRCUS OF HADRIAN.

NERO'S WARDROBE – (3.1) The Church of Sant' Andrea in Vaticano became the sacristy of Saint Peter's. Hence, perhaps, the idea of *Vestiarium.* Bunsen, *Beschreibung* 2.1: 39. Text reads *"Quod fuit vestiarium Neronis."*

NOVATIAN BATHS – (1.6) Known in ecclesiastical history (*Acta Santa Prassede,* 19 May, 295).

O

Orphan House – (3.13) *In orphanotrophio.* A church called *S. Stephani orphanotrophii,* also called in *schola cantorum,* is mentioned in old documents. Cencius, in Mabillon, *Museum Italicum* 2: 194; Zaccagni, Mai. *Spicilegium Romanorum* 9: 462.

P

Palace of Alexander – See Alexandrine Baths.

Palace of Antoninus – (1.7, 3.8) The ruins near the Column of Antoninus. *Columna Antonini in palatio suo.* [v-6]

Palace of Caligula – See Circus of Caligula.

Palace of Camillus – (1.7) *Palatium Camilli,* otherwise *Camillanum* (3.6) and *Campus Camilianus,* was the site of the ancient monastery of Saints Cyriac and Nicolas, now apparently absorbed in the Convent of Santa Marta (founded 1546) near the Collegio Romano. An arch called Arcus Camilli, crossing the Via del Piè di Marmo at the northwest corner of the convent is shown in Bufalini's plan dated 1502. [v-7]

Palace of Catiline – (3.10) Probably the ruin of the Temple of Castor. Suetonius mentions Catiline's house on the Palatine (*De grammaticis et rhetoribus* 17). [v-8]

PALACE OF CHROMATIUS – (1.7, 3.15) Chromatius (*praefectus urbis,* A.D. 284) was known by the *Acta* of Saint Sebastian, in which his palace and its destruction are described. (*Acta Sanctorum,* Bolland, 10 January). See Nichols, *Mirabiliana,* p. 169. Krautheimer (p. 243) places it at the eastern end of the Via dei Banchi Vecchi near Santa Lucia del Gonfalone. See also SANTO STEFANO IN PISCINULA. [V-9]

PALACE OF CLAUDIUS – (1.7) On the site of the *Domus Aurea* between the COLOSSEUM and SAN PIETRO IN VINCOLI. [V-10]

PALACE OF CONSTANTINE – The first mention in 1.7 is the LATERAN PALACE; the second in 1.7 was probably the Baths of Constantine [III-5] on the QUIRINAL, the ruins of which were opposite the Church of San Silvestro a Monte Cavallo. See also 3.14.

PALACE OF DIOCLETIAN – See BATHS OF DIOCLETIAN.

PALACE OF DOMITIAN – (1.7) *Palatium Domitiani in transtiberim ad micam auream.* A place called *mica aurea* occurs in the *Einsiedeln Itinerary* (Urlichs, p. 73); and is apparently in Trastevere. A church, San Giovanni in Mica Aurea on the Gianicolo, occurs in the fourteenth century. Santi Cosma e Damiano in Mica Aurea is now San Cosimata. See SAN GIOVANNI IN JANICULUM; Gregorovius 3: 525 and n. 1; Urlichs, p. 17. Perhaps it is the same as Montorio, a name said to be derived from the yellow sand found there. [V-11]

PALACE OF EUPHIMIANUS – (1.7) A house, possibly Roman, on the side of the Aventine facing the Tiber, consisting of a summer and winter palace, the former adjoining the Church of Santi Bonifacio ed Alessio. See Krautheimer, p. 255. [V-12]

PALACE OF LENTULUS – (3.15) The name is derived from an inscription (P. LENTULUS CN. F. SCIPIO, etc.) formerly on an arch near the Church of Santa Maria in Cosmedin or in *SCHOLA GRAECA*. Urlichs, p. 226.

PALACE OF NERO – (1.7) See LATERAN PALACE; (3.1) at the Vatican, see CIRCUS OF CALIGULA.

PALACE OF OCTAVIAN – (1.7) *Palatium Octaviani* probably alludes to the legend of Aracoeli (see 2.1); the mention of SAN LORENZO IN LUCINA is an addition, which associates this palace with the ARCH OF OCTAVIAN mentioned in 1.4.

PALACE OF ROMULUS – See TEMPLE OF ROMULUS.

PALACE OF SEVERUS – (1.7) Unidentified. Perhaps from the order in which it is named, the author may be referring to some ruin between the PALATINE and the COLOSSEUM.

PALACE OF TIBERIUS – (3.14) From the order in which it is named, it seems to have been on the QUIRINAL.

PALACE OF TITUS AND VESPASIAN – (1.7) In the description of Rome by the Jewish traveler, Benjamin of Tudela, the Palace of Titus is outside the walls.

PALACE OF TRAJAN AND HADRIAN – (1.7, 3.8) The pillar nearby (1.7) is the COLUMN OF TRAJAN; the Palace of Trajan in 3.14 is probably the TEMPLE OF TRAJAN in the FORUM OF TRAJAN [V-13]. *Pene totum lapidibus constructum* in 3.8 – probably marble is meant. For the temple before the gate (3.14), see 3.8, the TEMPLE OF THE GODDESS JUNO and the FORUM OF TRAJAN. Section

1.12 refers to the Tiberian Palace of Trajan, which is unidentified.

PALATINE HILL – (3.11) Between the ROMAN FORUM and the CIRCUS MAXIMUS. At 1.5, the Palatine Hill is called *Pallanteum,* in allusion to Virgil, *Aeneid* 8:53:

> *Delegere locum, et posuere in montibus urbem*
> *Pallantis proavi de nomine Pallanteum.*

THE PANTHEON – (1.6, 1.8, 2.4, 3.6) Built by Agrippa and rebuilt by Hadrian, also called Santa Maria Rotonda and Santa Maria ad Martyres. It was consecrated by Pope Boniface IV probably in the year 610 (*Liber Pontificialis*; Nibly, *Roma Moderna* 1: 407). The day kept as the dedication day is 13 May, but the festival of 1 November (All Saints Day) is believed to have been first celebrated in Rome as the feast of the Blessed Mother of God and of all the Martyrs. It was made a general festival for the whole church by Gregory IV. Usuardus, *Martyrologie in Acta Sanctorum,* vol. 26; Baronius, *Martyrologie Rom.* 1 Nov. See also Rosenstock-Hussey.

The two legends in 2.4, are not necessarily connected. The legend of the bells, known as *Salvatio Romae,* is at least as old as the eighth century, being narrated in Greek by Cosmas of Jerusalem (*Commentarium ad S. Gregorium Nazianzen,* Mai. *Spicilegium Romanum,* 2. 221; Urlichs, p. 179), and in a Latin book *De septem mundi miraculis,* attributed to Bede and found in a manuscript of that century (*Bede's Works,* ed. Giles 4: 10; Graf 1: 112, 189; see also Jordan 2: 366). The other legend, of Agrippa and Cybele, does not seem to be found in any earlier work.

The story (3.2, 3.6) of the Pigna having been on the Pantheon probably came from the name of the region (Rione della Pigna), in which the Pantheon was the principle building. The Pine Cone is now in the Giardino della Pigna at the Vatican. The supply of water through the nuts is spoken of as a thing of the past; but, as far as Nichols could see (p. 74), the Pigna did not give evidence of having been used in this way. He refers the reader, however, to Lancianni, *Atti dell' Accademia dei Lincei,* 10: 513.

The description of the Pantheon (foind in 3.2 and 3.6) contains a reminiscence of the tiles of gilded bronze, which were taken away by the Byzantine Emperor Constans II in 663.

PIAZZA NAVONA – See ALEXANDER'S THEATER.

PILLAR OF ANTONINUS – See COLUMN OF ANTONINUS.

PILLAR OF TRAJAN – See COLUMN OF TRAJAN.

PONTE MILVIO – (1.9) Ponte Molle, Milvian Bridge, or Pons Milvius; the northernmost bridge, crossing the Tiber at the Via Flaminia.

PONTE SANT' ANGELO – (1.9) Hadrian's Bridge; the ancient Pons Aelius or Pons Adrianus at CASTEL SANT' ANGELO. [1-10]

PONTE SANTA MARIA – See SENATORS' BRIDGE.

PONTE SISTO – See BRIDGE OF ANTONINUS.

PONTIAN CEMETERY – (1.11) South of the city on the Via Portuensis. See Krautheimer, p. 55.

PORTA APPIA – (1.3) The modern Porta San Sebastiano; in the south of the city leading into the Via Appia.

PORTA ASINARIA – See LATERAN GATE.

PORTA AURELIA – (1.3) The modern Porta San Pancrazio on the Janiculum, in the west of the city leading into the Via Aurelia. Also called Porta del Gianicolo.

PORTA CASTEL SANT' ANGELO – (1.3) The gate that closed the passage of the PONTE SANT' ANGELO.

PORTA COLLINA – (1.3) A gate in the Servian Wall near CASTEL SANT' ANGELO.

PORTA FLAMINIA – (1.3) On the site now occupied by the Porta del Popolo.

PORTA LABICANA – See PORTA PRENESTINA.

PORTA LATINA – (1.3, 1.11) The modern Porta Latina, near the BATHS OF CARACALLA, opening to the Via Latina.

PORTA METRONIA – (1.3) Between the BATHS OF CARACALLA and SAN GIOVANNI IN LATERANO. Originally in the Aurelian Wall.

PORTA NOMENTANA – (1.3) Just east of Porta Pia. It opened into the road leading to Nomentum, now Metana, 20 km northeast of Rome.

PORTA PINCIANA -(1.3) At the north end of the Via Veneto, formerly Porta Belisaria. A *Domus Pinciana* existed in a ruinous condition in the time of Theodoric. Cassiodorus (*Variae Epistolae* 3. 10) gives the form of an order for the removal to Ravenna of some of its marble materials. Nothing more is known of its history. Considerable remains appear in the medieval plans.

Porta Portese – (1.3) On the right bank of the Tiber at Ponte Aventino.

Porta Prenestina – (1.3) Porta Maggiore or Porta Labicana; leads east into Via Prenestina. It is formed by the archways of aqueducts carrying water from the Acqua Claudia and the Anio Novus.

Porta Salaria – (1.3) A northern gate in the Aurelian Wall leading into the Via Salaria.

Porta San Pancrazio – (1.3) See Porta Aurelia.

Porta San Sebastiano – See Porta Appia.

Porta Septimiana – (1.3) In the Aurelian Wall on the right bank of the Tiber near Ponte Sisto, or Bridge of Antoninus, and the Museo Torlonia. *Septem Naiades iunctae Iano.* These word, which were suggested by Ovid (*Metamorphoses* 14.785), appear to be introduced to supply an etymology for the name *Septimiana.* The later copies substitute the words *ubi septem laudes fuerunt factae Octaviano* (where seven praises were made for Octavian).

Porta Taurina – (1.3) Porta San Lorenzo or the Gate of Tivoli; at the meeting of the Via Tiburtina, Viale Labicana and Viale Tiburtino behind the Stazione Termini.

Porta Viridaria – (1.3) Now represented by the Porta Angelica. The name was derived from the *viridarium* or garden, which was behind the Vatican Palace and which was surrounded with a new wall by Pope Nicholas III in 1278. See an ancient inscription preserved in the Palazzo dei Conservatori on the Capitoline; and De Rossi, *Piante,* p. 83.

THE PYRAMID OF CESTIUS – (1.3) The Sepulcher or Temple of Remus at Porta San Paolo leading into the Via Ostiense [II-15]. Called the Sepulcher of Remus, just as the pyramid that formerly stood near the CASTEL SANT' ANGELO was called the Sepulcher of Romulus. See PYRAMID OF ROMULUS.

THE PYRAMID OF ROMULUS – (3.3) The Sepulcher of Romulus at CASTEL SANT' ANGELO. The pyramid, which in the fifth or sixth century was believed to be the Sepulcher of Scipio Africanus (Arco, *Schol. ad Horaces Epodes* 9.25), and in the twelfth was called *Meta* or *Sepulcrum Romuli,* was destroyed by Pope Alexander VI according to a note inserted on the great Mantuan plan published by De Rossi (*Piante,* tav. vi-xii). It stood on part of the present site of the church and monastery of Santa Maria Transpontina, the old church having been nearer the Mausoleum of Hadrian. Its position is well ascertained by the medieval plans of Rome and by the plan of Bufalini.

Some remains of ancient *opus quadratum* of tufo, used to repair the wall of the corridor, leading from the Vatican Palace to the Castle, close to the Via della Porta del Castello, are probably the result of the demolition of the pyramid. The outer casing of marble or travertine had been removed before, as appears from the text.

The corridor, which seems to have been formed on the ancient wall by Innocent VII and repaired by Alexander VI, is called *ambulatorium Alexandri sexti* in Bufalini's plan with his arms, with the date 1492, over the entrance to the quarters of the Swiss Guard.

Habuit circa se plateam Tiburtinam viginti pedum cum cloaca et florali suo. The pyramid in its dismantled state was called Saint Peter's Corn Heap *(acervus segatis S. Petri)* by the less learned pilgrims. It was said to have turned into a hill of stone when Nero took possession of it. Higden 1:230. [II-16]

Q

THE QUIRINAL – (1.5) The northernmost of the Seven Hills. Not the same hill as the AVENTINE, despite the text. Sant' Alessio and SANTA SABA are on the AVENTINE.

R

RIPARMEA – (1.9) On the right bank of the Tiber between Ponte Palatino and Ponte Aventino. According to Jordan (2: 195), it should be *Ripa Romea,* a medieval name for the Ripa Grande.

ROMAN ARCH – (1.2, 2.8) Section 1.2 locates this arch, where Constantine departed from Silvester II and Rome, between the AVENTINE and ALBISTON. [II-13, IV-11]

ROMAN FORUM – Section (3.10) leads the visitor from the south side of the CAPITOLINE, across the Roman Forum and up the Sacra Via. It should be noted that the names of these famous places appear to have been forgotten. [I-2]

ROUND SAINT MARY'S – See the PANTHEON and SANTA MARIA IN AQUIRO.

S

SANT' ADRIANO – (3.9) The SENATE HOUSE or Temple of Refuge in the Roman Forum; between 625 and 638 Pope Honorius converted it into this church with only minor structural changes. Krautheimer, p. 72.

SANT' AGATA AD GIROLUM – See CEMETERY OF SANT' AGATA.

SANT' AGATA DEI GOTI – (1.5) On Via Mazzarino, south of Via Nazionale and east of the Villa Aldobrandini.

SANT' ANASTASIO – See TRE FONTANE.

SANT' ANDREA IN VATICANO – See NERO'S WARDROBE.

SANT' ANTONIO – (3.10) Nothing is known of this church, which appears to have disappeared before the description was written. In the lower part of the great ruin behind the Temple of Castor, however, some religious paintings have been found.

SANT' APOLLINARE – (1.11) Near the Appian Gate, not the church north of Piazza Navona in the CAMPO MARZIO.

SANTA BALBINA IN ALBISTON – (1.12) In Parco di Porta Capena.

SAN BASILIO – (3.8) An ancient monastery built in the ruins of the Temple of Mars Ultor in the Forum of Augustus, was later the Convent of the Sisters of Sant' Annunziata.

Infra hunc terminum. The monastery was partly enclosed by the lofty wall of the Forum of Augustus, which was continued to the south by that of the FORUM OF NERVA. The former forum had lost its name, and the name of Trajan was extended over a wider area. So Petrus Mallius, *Ecclesia S. Basilii iuxta palatium Traiani imperatoris* (Mabillon 2: 161).

Jordan (2: 470) suggests that the story of the bronze tablet, which the writer does not seem to have seen, may have arisen from an inscription formerly existing by the Church of San Basilio (*Corpus Inscriptionum Latinorum* 1: 278):

C. IULIUS CAESAR STRABO AED. CUR...IUD. PONTIF.

See Macc. 80:22, for the league between the Romans and the Jews.

SAN CAESARIO – (3.11) There may have been a church of that name on the PALATINE in addition to the well-known church on the Via Appia.

SANTA CROCE IN GERUSALEMME – (1.7, 3.13) Basilica Sessoriana, or Susurrian Palace; south of the Porta Maggiore (PORTA PRENESTINA); founded by Saint Helena and enriched with relics brought by her from Jerusalem. *Palatium quod appellatur Sessorium* existed in Theodoric' time. (*Excerpta Valesiana,* in Ammianus Marcellinus, *Rerum gestarum libri qui supersunt,* ed. V. E. Gardthausen 2: 298.). The Einsiedeln traveler, going eastward across the ruined city, passed first *palatium iuxta iherusalem,* and then *Hierusalem.* (*Einsiedeln Itinerary,* Urlichs, p. 73). [V-15]

SAN CYRIACO – (3.6) A church by this name existed on the Corso near the present Palazzo Doria.

SANTI FABIANO E SEBASTIANO – (1.11) Near the Cemetery of Callisto.

SANTA FRANCESCA ROMANA – See SANTA MARIA NOVA.

SAN GIOVANNI IN GIANICOLO – (1.1) This church in Trastevere appears to have been the same as San Giovanni in Mica Aurea. See Krautheimer, p. 246, fig. 193b and p. 247.

SAN GIOVANNI IN LATERANO – (2.8, 3.13) One of the seven major churches of Rome, at the LATERAN GATE.

SAN GIOVANNI IN MICA AUREA – See SAN GIOVANNI IN GIANICOLO.

SAN LORENZO IN LUCINA – (1.4, 1.7) Behind Palazzo Fiano on the Corso.

SAN LORENZO IN MIRANDA – (3.10) Temple of Antoninus and Faustinus in the ROMAN FORUM.

SAN LORENZO FUORI LE MURA – (1.11) East of the Stazione Termini outside the city walls. [1-18]

SAN LORENZO IN PANISPERNA – (1.6) On Via Panisperna between the Basilica of SANTA MARIA MAGGIORE and Villa Aldobrandini.

SANTE LUCA E MARTINA – (1.4, 3.9) Santa Martina; opposite the MAMERTINE PRISON.

SAN MARCO – (3.6) Part of Palazzo Venezia.

SANTA MARIA IN AQUIRO – (1.4) Or Santa Maria Rotonda; in the region of the PANTHEON, just west of the Corso and south of Palazzo Montecitorio. It was a church prior to 750 with a hospital. See Gregorovius 2: 247; Krautheimer, p. 74, 252, and 278.

SANTA MARIA IN ARACOELI – (2.1, 3.7) On the CAPITOLINE. Until the thirteenth century the proper name of the church continued to be Santa Maria in Capitolio (Gregorovius 4: 545). Jordan (2: 366) suggests that the authority of the *Mirabilia* may have led to the official recognition of the name connected with the legend in 2.1. The Franciscans were established here in 1250, twenty-five years after Saint Francis's death. They still retain the church.

SANTA MARIA IN CAMPO – (3.8) Placed in Bufalini's plan on the slope of the QUIRINAL, a little south of SANT' AGATA. However, the Church of Santa Maria in Campo Carleone existed until the late nineteenth century at the western end of the south side of the existing Via Campo Carleone. See Nolli's plan dated 1748.

SANTA MARIA IN CATARINO – (3.15) Unidentified. See CIRCUS OF ANTONINUS.

SANTA MARIA IN FONTANA – See TEMPLE OF FAUNUS.

SANTA MARIA MAGGIORE – (1.5, 3.14) The basilica on the ESQUILINE; one of the seven major Roman churches.

SANTA MARIA NOVA – (1.4, 1.7, 3.10) Also known as Santa Francesca Romana; in front of the TEMPLE OF VENUS AND ROME at the east end of the ROMAN FORUM.

SANTA MARIA IN PALLARA – See TEMPLE OF PALLAS.

SANTA MARIA ROTONDA – See the PANTHEON and SANTA MARIA IN AQUIRO.

SANTA MARIA IN TRASTEVERE – (1.12, 3.16) In Piazza Santa Maria in Trastevere.

SANTA MARTINA – See SANTE LUCA E MARTINA.

SAN NEREO – See SANTI NEREO ED ACHILLEO.

SANTI NEREO ED ACHILLEO – (1.12) *Felix III. Romanus de titulo Fasciolae. Lib. Pontif., in vita Felicis III.* See Fasciola. [IV-3]

SAN NICOLA IN CARCERE – (3.15) Stands on the site of three ancient temples in the Forum Holitorium, between the CAPITOLINE and the Tiber. One temple is of unknown dedication, the others were dedicated to Juno Sospita and Spes (*Blue Guide,* p. 82). The church acquired, by an erroneous association of names, the title, *in carcere Tulliano.* From this it was an easy step to Cicero. Pierleone, father of Pope Anacletus II, died in 1128. His house under the Capitol *(qua Capitolii rupes aedibus Petri Leonis imminet, Vita Paschalis II)* was near San Nicola and probably included the remains of the Theater of Marcellus. See TEMPLE OF CICERO AT THE TULLIANUM.

SAN PAOLO FUORI LE MURA – (2.8) On Via Ostiense. The body of Saint Paul lies in the Catacombs of Commodilla, or Garden of Lucina (1.12) [IV-6], near San Paolo fuori le Mura, despite the fact that the text (1.12) claims that it lies at San Paolo fuori le Mura. De Rossi, *Roma Sotterranea* 1: 185; *Acta Sanctorum,* June, 7: 488.

Saint Peter's Needle – (1.7, 3.1) The Vatican Obelisk in Piazza San Pietro. It was popularly called Saint Peter's Needle, *acus,* or *agulia, S. Petri.* A careless reading of the dedicatory inscription to Augustus and Tiberius (the Latin letters referred to in the text):

DIVO . CAESARI . DIVI . IVLII . F . AVGVSTO
TI . CAESARI . DIVI . AVGVSTI . F . AVGVSTO
SACRVM

may have led to its being taken for a memorial of Caesar. *Memoria Caesaris, id est Agulia.* The word *Agulia* or *Guglia* was also suggestive of *Julia* or *columna Julia.* Compare Suetonius, *Iulius* 85, upon which the narrative (3.1) of the twelfth century was based. *Columpnam ei solidam lapidis Numidici XX prope pedum in foro statuerunt, super quam tumulatus, quae Iulia dicta est. Chron. S Pantaleonis,* Johann G. von Eckhart, *Corpus Historicum Medii Aevi,* 2: 695; Urlichs, p. 181.

Et litteris latinis decenter depicta. Before the present bronze ornaments of eagles and festoons were attached in 1723, the holes to which the ancient decorations had been added were visible. Fontana, *Obelisco,* p. 8. The bronze lions, which appear to sustain the obelisk, date from the time of its removal under Sixtus v. But it was constantly stated before its removal that it rested on four bronze lions (Higden 1: 226; Petrarch, *Familiares* 6.2). Higden tells us that there was a saying among the pilgrims that a person free from mortal sin could creep under that stone. Bunsen (2: 157) denies that the ancient supports were really lions.

The following verses are the beginning of an epitaph or poem referred by William of Malmesbury (p. 212) to Emperor Henry III (d. 1056). See also Jordan 2: 373; Graf 1: 296:

> *Caesar, tantus eras quantus et orbis:*
> *Sed nunc in modico clauderis antro.*

The following epigram is added in a manuscript of the fourteenth century. The Latin lines may have been written in Greek letters to excite curiosity.

> *Si lapis est unus, dic qua sit arte levatus;*
> *Et si sint plures, dic ubi contigui.*

SAINT PETER'S PARADISE – (1.2, 1.3, 3.2) Also Saint Peter's Porch or Saint Peter's Parvise (see p. xii). The Paradise of Saint Peter's was the atrium in front of the basilica. From Anastasius on the life of Symmachus: *Cantharum beati Petri cum quadriporticu marmoribus ornavit, et ex musivo fecit agnos et cruces et palmas. Ipsum vero atrium marmoribus compaginavit: gradus vero ante fores basilicae b. Petri ampliavit. Liber Pontificialis.*

The Pine Cone is now in the Giardino della Pigna at the Vatican. The supply of water through the pine nuts is spoken of (3.2) as a thing of the past. It is doubtful whether the *Pigna* ever had this function, but see Lanciani, *Atti dell' Accademia dei Lincei,* 10: 513. See also the PANTHEON.

SAINT PETER'S PORCH – See SAINT PETER'S PARADISE.

SANTA PETRONILLA – (3.1) *Quod dicitur Sancta Petronilla.* The Church of Saint Parnel, or Santa Petronilla, was a round building where the apse on the south side of Saint Peter's is now. Martinelli, p. 384.

SAN PIETRO IN VINCOLI – (1.7, 2.6, 3.14) *Ad vincula*; just south of Via Cavour in the ancient Subura. It was founded by Eudoxia, the wife of the Emperor Valentinian III, who is confused in the legend with Eudoxia, the wife of Arcadius. The feast day of the dedication of this church, 1 August, was observed in antiquity as a festival in memory of the death of Antony. *1 Aug. Feriae ob necem Antonii. Fasti in Corpus Inscriptionum Latinorum,* 1: 376

According to legend, Juvenal, bishop of Jerusalem, gave two sets of chains to the Empress Eudoxia, wife of Theodosius the Younger. One set she placed in Constantinople, the other she sent to her daughter, Eudoxia, wife of Valentinian III. The Roman set and the

Constantinople set, which was sent to Rome at a later date, were both Peter's, and they were miraculously joined together when they were reunited. [I-17]

SAN QUIRICO – (1.12, 3.8) In the Via Tor dei Conti.

SANTA SABA – (1.5, 3.11) On the Piccolo Aventino.

SANTA SABINA – (1.4) On the AVENTINE.

SAN SALVATORE – (3.6) *Iuxta Sanctum Salvatorem.* The reading is uncertain, since it might be associated with the PALACE OF ANTONINUS or with SANTA MARIA IN AQUIRO. The church is not known. San Salvatore in Coppelle was founded in 1195, later than the *Mirabilia.* Martinelli, p. 398.

SAN SALVATORE DE STATERA – (3.9) The origin of the church's name is unknown. It seems to have been on the south side of the CAPITOLINE (Jordan 2: 483-87), possibly the church now called Sant' Omobono, formerly San Salvatore in Porticu. Martinelli, p. 391. It is impossible to say what foundation there may have been for the story of an arch, which, it should be observed, is not spoken of as existing. Perhaps the whole story was suggested by the additional name of the church.

SAN SERGIO – (3.9) Removed between 1539 and 1551; stood on the south corner of the ruins of the TEMPLE OF CONCORD. (Nichols, *Notizie dei Rostri,* pp. 65-71.) The ancient ascent is spoken of in the past tense.

SAN SISTO – (1.7) East of the BATHS OF CARACALLA.

SANTO STEFANO ALLE CARROZZE – See SANTO STEFANO ROTONDO.

SANTO STEFANO IN MONTE CAELIO – See SANTO STEFANO ROTONDO.

SANTO STEFANO IN PISCINULA – (3.15) Stood opposite Santa Lucia in the Via Santa Lucia.

SANTO STEFANO ROTONDO – (1.5) Santo Stefano in Monte Caelio, the largest circular church in the world, located on the Caelian Hill. See also SCIPIO'S TEMPLE.

The Round Saint Stephen of the twelfth century (3.15) was Santo Stefano alle Carrozze, commonly known as the TEMPLE OF VESTA, in the Piazza Bocca di Verità.

See also TEMPLE OF FAUNUS.

SANTA SUSANNA – (1.6) On Via Venti Settembre, between the BATHS OF DIOCLETIAN and Palazzo Barberini.

SANTA TRINITA – (1.12) Unidentified; does not match either the Santa Trinità on the Pincian or in the Campo dei Fiori. *Et insula catenata post sanctam Trinitatem.*

SANT' URSO – (1.4) Near the PONTE SANT' ANGELO. If the Church of Sant' Urso in 3.6 is the same one, then the pilgrim makes a fresh start here in the perambulation of the city.

SAN VALENTINO – (1.3) An ancient church, repaired by Leo III (795-816), outside the Porta del Popolo near Ponte Milvio. See Krautheimer, pp. 54, 312.

SANTA VIVIANA – (1.11) Santa Bibiana near Porta San Lorenzo.

SASSIA – (1.9) Between San Pietro in Vaticano and CASTEL SANT' ANGELO. In the early Middle Ages the locality now called Borgo di Santo Spirito in Sassia was known as the *Vicus Saxonum* or *Saxonia,* owing to the foundation there of a *Schola Saxonum* by Ini, king of the West Saxons, in 727 and of a hospital for pilgrims by Offa, king of Mercia, in 794.

SCHOLA GRAECA – (3.15) At Santa Maria in Cosmedin in the Piazza Bocca di Verità.

SCIPIO'S TEMPLE – (3.13) Nothing is known about this ruin, unless it is SANTO STEFANO ROTONDO on the Caelian Hill.

SENATE – (1.5) Also Senators' Palace; restored in name in 1143 and installed on the CAPITOLINE, probably in the ancient Tabularium. See Gregorovius 4: 519, 550. De Rossi has called attention to a document dated 1150, *in capitolio in consistorio novo palatii. Chron. Pisan*; Muratori 4: 171. See also SANT' ADRIANO. [V-14]

SENATORS' BRIDGE – The Ponte Rotto, south of the Tiber Island; also called Ponte Santa Maria from the Church of Santa Maria Egiziaca (see THE GRATINGS). The ancient Pons Aemilius. See Hibbert, p. 331. [I-15]

SENATORS' PALACE – See SENATE.

SEPTIZONIUM – (1.8, 1.12, 2.5, 3.11) Temple of the Sun and Moon, also Seven Floors; probably in the southeast corner of the PALATINE, at the eastern end of the Belvedere. [V-18]

SEPULCHER OF AUGUSTUS – See MAUSOLEUM OF AUGUSTUS.

SEPULCHER OF HADRIAN – (3.4) Now the sepulcher of Pope Innocent in the Lateran. The cover is in Saint Peter's Porch on the tomb of the prefect Cinthius or Cencius, who died in 1079. Gregorovius 4: 245.

SEPULCHER OF JULIUS CAESAR – (1.7, 3.1) SAINT PETER'S NEEDLE.

SEPULCHER OF REMUS – See PYRAMID OF CESTIUS.

SEPULCHER OF ROMULUS – See PYRAMID OF ROMULUS.

SEVEN FLOORS – See SEPTIZONIUM.

SEVERIAN AND COMMODIAN BATHS – (3.11) *Thermae Severianae et Commodianae.* From the *Notitia,* Region 1, *Porta Capena.* The locality is probably arbitrary.

SHELL OF PARIONE – (3.6) The *Concha Parionis* was probably an antique basin in the region of Parione. Before the beginning of the fourteenth century it had been removed to the hospital of Saint James at the Colosseum. *Anonymus Magliabecchianus,* Urlichs, p. 163.

SILVERSMITHS' HILL – See HILL OF THE SILVERSMITHS.

STADIUM – See CIRCUS MAXIMUS.

STADIUM OF SEVERUS ALEXANDER – See ALEXANDER'S THEATER.

STEPS OF ELIOGABALUS – See GRADUS ELIOGABALI.

SUSURRIAN PALACE – See SANTA CROCE IN GERUSALEMME.

T

TARPEIAN HILL – See CAPITOLINE.

TEMPLE OF AELIAN HADRIAN – (3.6) Unidentified; near SANTA MARIA IN AQUIRO.

TEMPLE OF AESCULAPIUS – (3.10) There is some evidence of this ancient temple near the COLOSSEUM (Jordan 2: 508). There was also a Temple of Aesculapius (3.16) on the Tiber Island (Gregorovius 3: 483). [V-19]

TEMPLE OF APOLLO – (3.1, 3.6, 3.12, 3.14) The temples in 3.6 and 3.12 are unknown. The one in 3.14 in the PALACE OF DIOCLETIAN appears to be imaginary; see THE BUSHELS. See CIRCUS OF CALIGULA for the temple at the Vatican (3.1).

TEMPLE OF ASILIS – (3.7) On the CAPITOLINE; unidentified. "I did enact Julius Caesar; I was killed i' the Capitol." Shakespeare, *Hamlet* 3. 2. Perhaps a remote example of the influence of Mirabilian legend.

TEMPLE OF ASYLUM – See TEMPLE OF ROMULUS.

TEMPLE OF BACCHUS – (3.8) On the Sacra Via opposite the Basilica of Constantine; (3.15) at TOWER OF CENCIUS DE ORRIGO [V-16].

TEMPLE OF BELLONA – (3.6) Unidentified; an example of the author's propensity to convert all ancient ruins to temples.

TEMPLE OF CARMENTIS – (3.7) On the CAPITOLINE; (3.8) at SAN BASILIO. [V-20]

TEMPLE OF CICERO AT THE TULLIANUM – The original text (3.15), without an addition from the *Graphia,* runs as follows: *et templum Ciceronis in Tulliano est* [or *et*] *templum Iovis ubi fuit pergula aurea.* See TEMPLE OF JUPITER and SAN NICOLA IN CARCERE.

TEMPLE OF CONCORD – (1.4, 3.9) At the western end of the ROMAN FORUM *(Iuxta aerarium publicum)* behind the CAPITOLINE. The situation of the temples of Concord and Saturn (the *aerarium*) and of the *clivus Capitolinus* appears to have been rightly known. See also TEMPLE OF VESPASIAN. [V-20]

TEMPLE OF CONCORD AND PIETY – See TEMPLE OF PIETY AND CONCORD.

TEMPLE OF CONCORD AND SATURN – (3.8) On the HILL OF THE SILVERSMITHS. See also the TEMPLE OF VESPASIAN. [V-21]

TEMPLE OF CRATICULA – (3.15) The building called the Temple of Craticula was a little west of the Portico of Octavia. See Nichols, *Mirabiliana,* p. 159. The Region of Arenula (Rione della Regola) appears to have also been called *regio caccabariorum,* and the Church of Santa Maria de Pianto to have been San Salvatore Cacabari. Cencius in Mabillon, *Museum Italicum,* p. 193; Martinelli, *Roma Sacra,* p. 388; *Nomina ecclesiarum saec. xiv,* Urlichs, pp. 170, 174. This church is said to have been at the entrance of the Temple of Craticula. *Anonymus Magliabecchianus,* Urlichs, p. 169. [V-22]

TEMPLE OF CYBELE – (3.14) An unidentified temple said to be near the COLOSSEUM. Obviously not the one on the PALATINE below the ruins of the *Domus Tiberiana.*

TEMPLE OF DIVES ANTONINUS – (3.6) In PALACE OF ANTONINUS.

TEMPLE OF DIVINE HADRIAN – (3.8) Perhaps the remains of the Basilica Ulpia and the TEMPLE OF TRAJAN; not the Temple of Hadrian whose ruins were incorporated into the Borsa. [V-23]

TEMPLE OF THE FABII – (3.9) The Fabian Arch probably stood at the west corner of the Temple of Faustina. But the name of Fabius appears to have migrated to the neighborhood of the MAMERTINE PRISON.

TEMPLE OF FAUNUS – (3.14, 3.15) An unidentified temple said to be at Santa Maria in Fontana; mentioned in the Liber *Pontificalis. Leo III,* sect. 362. The legend that Julian was led astray by the speech of an idol in the Temple of Faunus is not found elsewhere. There is another legend that he took an idol of Mercury out of the Tiber, and the demon within it induced him to renounce Christianity and gave him the empire. *Kaiserchronik,* cited by Graf 2: 136.

In Section 3.15 there is reference to a Temple of Faunus identified with SANTO STEFANO ROTONDO, which was the TEMPLE OF VENUS in the Piazza Bocca di Verità.

Ovid, Fasti 2.193:

Idibus agrestis fumant altaria Fauni,
Hic ubi discretas insula rumpit aquas.

TEMPLES OF FLORA AND PHOEBUS – (3.6) Imaginary; example of the author's propensity to convert all ancient ruins to temples.

TEMPLE OF FORTUNE – (3.11) A Temple of Fortune in front of the SEPTIZONIUM [V-18]; not the Temple of

Fortuna Virilis in the Piazza Bocca di Verità (Gregorovius 3: 560-61); see also THE GRATINGS.

TEMPLE OF FORTUNE AND DIANA – (3.16) The Temple of Fors Fortuna trans Tiberim was probably known to the author through Ovid (Fasti 6.773), but this one appears to have been outside the Ostian Gate. Becker, *Handbuch* 1: 479. [V-24]

TEMPLE OF THE GODDESS JUNO – (3.8) The Temple before the gate of the FORUM OF TRAJAN. See also PALACE OF TRAJAN.

TEMPLE OF THE GODS – *Templum deorum*: the names of the gods (3.14) were perhaps omitted by oversight.

TEMPLE OF GORGON – (3.16) *Templum Gorgonis.* In the Notitia, Region 14. In *Transtiberina,* a monument called *Caput Gorgonis* is registered.

TEMPLE OF HERCULES – (3.7, 3.16) Unidentified; (3.13) at SANTA CROCE IN GERUSALEMME.

TEMPLE OF JANUS – (3.7, 3.10) The Temple of Janus may have been the TEMPLE OF VESPASIAN or possibly a ruin below the CHURCH OF SANTA MARIA IN ARACOELI, towards the MARMERTINE PRISON. According to Nichols, the Camellaria appears to have been in the ruins of the TEMPLE OF CONCORD. See the Bull of Anacletus II, Nichols, Mir*abiliana,* p. 179. Janus as *custos Capitolii* is a reminiscence of Ovid (*Fasti* 1.257-72). There is also a shrine of Janus near the steps of the Basilica Aemelia.

TEMPLE OF JUNO – (3.7) On the northern excrescence of the CAPITOLINE where the Church of SANTA MARIA IN ARACOELI now stands. The text of 3.7 refers to the temple as over the BASILICA JULIA. See Krautheimer, p. 285. Temple in 3.11 is unidentified. [V-25]

TEMPLE OF JUPITER – (3.11) The GREATER PALACE on the PALATINE [V-3]; (3.16) on the Tiber Island. Sections 3.8 and 3.15 appear to refer to the Temple or Basilica of Jupiter [V-26] at the Portico of Octavia, in the Middle Ages called, from an inscription, the Severian Temple. *Pergola d'oro* may have been a popular name. In a twelfth century letter Sant' Angelo in Pescheria is called *Sant' Angeli iuxta templum Jovis.* The Acts of Saint Laurence mention the Basilica of Jupiter [IV-16] as part of the PALACE OF TIBERIUS (*Acta S. Laurentii* 10 Aug. 518). It is placed (3.8) at SAN QUIRICO in Via Tor dei Conti. In a processional order the name occurs near Piazza Montanara, near Theater of Marcellus. Nichols, *Mirabiliana,* p. 158; Gregorovius 4: 471, n. 1; 663 and n. 2. See also TEMPLE OF CICERO AT THE TULLIANUM.

TEMPLE OF JUPITER AND DIANA – See EMPEROR'S TABLE.

TEMPLE OF JUPITER AND MONETA – (2.4, 2.8, 3.7) On the south part of the CAPITOLINE overlooking the ROMAN FORUM. See Krautheimer, p. 285

TEMPLE OF MARS – (1.12, 3.9) The Temple of Mars Ultor in the Forum of Augustus [V-27]. The statue called *Marsorio,* removed in the sixteenth century to the Piazza del Campidoglio and the court of the Museo Capitolino in or about 1668. *Roma Antica e Moderna,* 1668 ed., p. 661. There was also the Temple of Mars (1.4, 1.12, 3.16), about two miles from the PORTA APPIA. Here Saint Sixtus was beheaded. *Acta S. Sixti,* 6 Aug. 140. See also *Acta S. Stephani,* 2 Aug. 141; *S. Cornelii* 14 Sept. 144. In the legendary *Acts of Pope Stephen* (Mombritius 2: 274) the temple fell upon the prayer of that saint.

Section 3.6 also notes a Temple of Mars in the CAMPO MARZIO. See also THE BUSHELS for the temple in 3.14.

TEMPLE OF MERCURY – (3.15) It appears one was on this side of the AVENTINE (Jordan 2: 530); and a Mercury's Well is mentioned in the *Einsiedeln Itinerary* as on the Aventine above Santa Maria in Cosmedin [V-28]. At 3.15 the writer probably had Ovid in mind (*Fasti* 5.669):

> *Templa tibi posuere patres spectantia circum*
> *Idibus: ex quo est haec tibi festa dies.*
> *Te, quicunque suas profitetur vendere merces*
> *Thure dato, tribuas ut sibi lucra, rogat.*

TEMPLE OF MINERVA CHALCIDICA – (3.6) Southeast of the PANTHEON where Santa Maria sopra Minerva was built [V-29]. This is an addition from Montfaucon's text, probably from the fourteenth century. A fifteenth century map shows some ruins adjoining the Church of Santa Maria sopra Minerva to the east (De Rossi, *Piante,* tav. iv). The small obelisk, now before the Pantheon, was in the little square before San Macuto until 1711 is not alluded to in the text. We may perhaps conclude that it was excavated at a later time. It is shown in a map of about 1475, when it had already acquired the legendary name of the Sepulcher of Brutus. See also TEMPLE OF NERVA.

TEMPLE OF NERVA – (3.8) The remains in the FORUM OF NERVA of the TEMPLE OF MINERVA, dedicated by Nerva [V-30]. The ruins were destroyed by Pope Paul V who used the stones for the Fontana Paola on the Gianicolo. Also mentioned are temples at SAN LORENZO IN MIRANDA (3.10) and at the GOLDEN VAIL (3.15).

TEMPLE OF PALLAS – (3.10) The Temple of Pallas in the ROMAN FORUM [V-31]; from the TEMPLE OF VESTA the visitor is conducted northward to the other side of the Roman Forum. The first building passed in this direction would include the marble walls of the Regia, perhaps the Temple of Pallas of the text. The Temple of Pallas before the Portico of Faustina is said to have been demolished under Paul III. (Magnan, *Città di Roma,* 1: 34). This was the time of the removal of the remains of the Regia.

The Temple of Pallas on the PALATINE (3.11, 3.15) is unidentified but linked in name to the monastery of San Sebastiano, also called Santa Maria in Pallara, still existing on the Palatine near the ARCH OF TITUS. It appears to have derived its name from an ancient *palladium palatinum* mentioned in an inscription of the time of Constantine. De Rossi, *Bulletino di. Archaeologia.* Cristiano, 1867, p. 15.

TEMPLE OF PEACE AND LATONA – (3.10) The Forum of Peace in the ROMAN FORUM, west of the Basilica of Constantine. Nichols believed it to be the same as the Basilica of Constantine. It was afterwards called the TEMPLE OF PEACE, and the TEMPLE or PALACE OF ROMULUS. See TEMPLE OF ROMULUS. The name *Latona* was derived from the learned name of an adjoining arch, popularly called the Arco del Latrone. See Nichols, *Mirabiliana,* p. 175; Urlichs, p. 106. [V-31]

TEMPLE OF PHOEBUS – See TEMPLES OF FLORA AND PHOEBUS.

TEMPLE OF PIETY AND CONCORD – (1.7, 3.10) The Temple of Concord and Piety; the double TEMPLE OF VENUS AND ROME behind the Church of SANTA MARIA NOVA or Santa Francesca Romana.

TEMPLE OF POMPEY – See THEATER OF POMPEY.

Temple of Ravennates – (1.12, 3.16) The name *urbs Ravennatium* – which occurs in some of the Acts of the Martyrs and has been thought to derive from some *castra Ravennatium* established in Trastevere, analogous to the *castra Misenatium* in the Third Region – suggested a Temple of Ravennates at Santa Maria in Trastevere. The legend of the fountain of oil and the name *taberna meritoria* are from the Chronicle of Jerome. Anno Abrah. 1976, *E taberna meritoria trans Tiberim oleum terra erupit fluxitque tota die sine intermissione, significans Christi gratiam ex gentibus. Ubi merebantur milites qui gratis serviebant in senatu.* [IV-20, V-32]

Temple of Refuge – See Sant' Adriano.

Temple of Remus – See Pyramid of Cestius.

Temple of Romulus – (1.7, 3.10) Palace of Romulus or Temple of Asylum. The ancient building to the west of the Basilica of Constantine appears to have joined the Forum of Peace. On the walls of this building the marble plan of Rome hung, which is partly preserved in the Museo Capitolino. Nichols believed the temple to be the same as the Basilica of Constantine. It is now, however, thought to be the round building in front of the Forum of Peace or Santi Cosma e Damiano. [V-31]

Temple of Saturn – (3.8, 3.9) Behind the Capitoline at the western end of the Roman Forum. See also Temple of Concord and Temple of Vespasian. For the Temple of Saturn in 3.14, see The Bushels.

Temple of Saturn and Bacchus – (3.14) The statues called Saturn and Bacchus were the two river gods now in the Piazza Campidoglio.

TEMPLE OF SIBYL – (3.15) Identified with Santa Maria in Cosmedin. [V-33]

TEMPLE OF THE SUN – (3.11) In front of the PALATINE, per-haps the TEMPLE OF THE SUN AND MOON, but probably not the same as 2.7 before the COLOSSEU; 3.15 is unidentified.

TEMPLE OF THE SUN AND MOON – (3.11) Also called the SEPTIZONIUM.

TEMPLE OF TITUS – (3.8) Unidentified; see SANTA MARIA IN CAMPO.

TEMPLE OF TRAJAN – (3.8) In the FORUM OF TRAJAN.

TEMPLE OF VENUS – (3.14) An unidentified temple near SAN PIETRO IN VINCOLI. For the Temple of Venus cited in 3.6, see the LIME-KILN.

TEMPLE OF VESPASIAN – (3.8) The temples of Concord, Saturn, Vespasian and Titus are from the *Notitia,* where they follow the Basilica Argentaria in the same order. But Concord and Saturn are paired together here in one temple, instead of Vespasian and Titus. Some of these temples appear again in the text.

TEMPLE OF VESTA – (3.10) In the ROMAN FORUM. The text also refers to a Temple of Vesta (3.6) in the region of the PANTHEON. There is reason to believe that considerable remains of the Temple of Vesta in Piazza Bocca di Verità existed above ground in the twelfth century, but the text does not mention it by name. See Lanciani, ser. 3, 10: 349. See also TEMPLE OF FAUNUS and SANTO STEFANO ROTONDO.

TEMPLE OF VESTA AND CAESAR – (3.7) On the CAPITOLINE; unidentified.

TEREBINTH OF NERO – (3.3) *Circa se habuit terbentinum (or terebinta) Neronis.* The Terebinth (η τερ εβιυθος) near the *NAUMACHIA* is mentioned in some Greek acts of Saints Peter and Paul. (*Acta Apochr.* ed. Tischendorf, p. 37, cited by Jordan 2: xvii). In an order for the emperor's coronation, probably of the eleventh century, Henry III is described as taking the oath to observe the rights of the Roman people at Santa Maria Transpontina, which is near the Terebinth. (Gregorovius 4: 59 and n. 2). It is perhaps the same monument that is called *obeliscus Neronis* in the ordo of Benedictus Canonicus. (See Nichols, *Mirabiliana,* Extracts 1 and 4.)

This seems to agree with the ecclesiastical tradition. *Acta SS. Petri et Pauli. Supervenit autem populus infinitus ad locum qui appellatur Naumachia iuxta obeliscum Neronis. Illic enim crux posita est.* Mombritius, f. 199.

It appears to have been destroyed in the twelfth century, since the *Mirabilia* records only an exaggerated tradition of its magnificence. The origin of its medieval name is obscure. The word denotes a turpentine tree, and among the local objects in the bas-relief of Saint Peter's crucifixion on the bronze door of Saint Peter's a tall tree between the Mausoleum of Hadrian and the Pyramid of Romulus appears to symbolize the Terebinth.

THEATER OF ANTONINUS – (1.8) The Theater of Balbus in the Ghetto, north of the Theater of Marcellus. See also CIRCUS OF ANTONINUS. [III-10]

THEATER OF BALBUS – See THEATER OF ANTONINUS.

THEATER OF POMPEY – (1.8) Behind the Church of Sant' Andrea della Valle; also called his temple. [III-15]

THEATER OF TARQUIN AND THE EMPERORS – See CIRCUS MAXIMUS.

THEATER OF TITUS AND VESPASIAN – (1.8) The Circus of Maxentius on the Via Appia. [III-17]

THREE CROSS WAYS – See TREVI.

TIBERIAN PALACE OF TRAJAN – See the PALACE OF TRAJAN.

TOFULA – (3.8) Santa Maria in Tofella is mentioned by Cencius (Mabillon 2: 192). The site is uncertain.

TOWER OF CENCIUS DE ORRIGO – (3.15) May have been the building on the *Janus Quadrifrons,* of which the remains appear in Piranesi's engraving and other views until the beginning of the nineteenth century. But the *Velum Aureum* occurs later in 3.15. [V-16]

TOWER OF TOSETTI – (1.4) The position of this tower is not identified except for its proximity to the ARCH OF ANTONINUS. The surname occurs elsewhere.

TRASO'S CEMETERY – See CEMETERY OF TRASO.

TRE FONTANE – Formerly Acqua Salvia; off the Via Laurentina near E.U.R. The church of Sant' Anastasio at Tre Fontane was given by Innocent II in 1140, about the date of the *Mirabilia,* to Saint Bernard, who founded a monastery of Cistercian monks there. Place of the martyrdom of Saint Paul. [IV-5]

TREVI – (3.14) Three Cross Ways; *In capite trivii,* the modern Trevi. Whether the name trivium is of classical origin is not certain.

TULLIAN PRISON – See SAN NICOLA IN CARCERE.

V

VALENTINIAN BRIDGE – (1.9) Jordan (2: 195) believes this was the same as that of Theodosius and that there were never more than two bridges below the island.

VICUS CANARIUS – (1.12) At San Giorgio in Velabro. [IV-4]

VICUS LATERICII – (1.12) The *Vicus Latericii* occurs only in connection with the Church of Santa Prasede on the ESQUILINE. [IV-14]

VICUS PATRICII – (1.12) The Vicus patricius was an ancient street and was famous in ecclesiastical tradition for the house of Pudens and the residence of Saint Peter. [IV-15]

VOLUSIAN PALACE – (1.7) Probably named not from the emperor but from a Volusian associated in the legend with the story of Pilate. Graf 1: 380, 392.

W

THE WALLS – Very full and curious details concerning the matters referred to in 1.2 are found at the end of the *Einsiedeln Itinerary* (Urlichs, p. 78; Jordan, 2: 578). There is no mention there of castles or chief arches. The exaggeration of the circuit of wall, which is common to other medieval descriptions, is thought by De Rossi

(*Piante di Roma,* p. 68) to have originated in a misapprehension of the measurements given by Pliny, *Historia Naturalis* 3.5, 66.

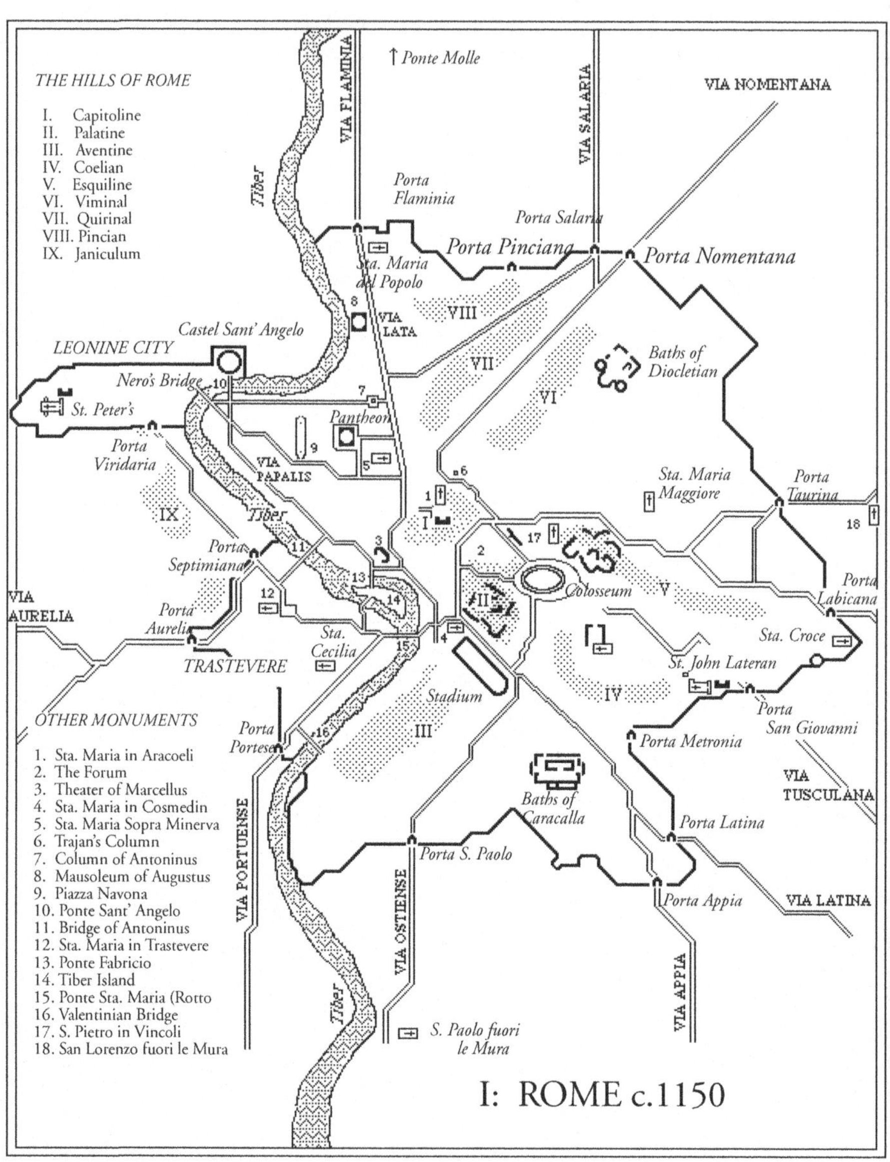
THE HILLS OF ROME
I. Capitoline
II. Palatine
III. Aventine
IV. Coelian
V. Esquiline
VI. Viminal
VII. Quirinal
VIII. Pincian
IX. Janiculum
OTHER MONUMENTS
1. Sta. Maria in Aracoeli
2. The Forum
3. Theater of Marcellus
4. Sta. Maria in Cosmedin
5. Sta. Maria Sopra Minerva
6. Trajan's Column
7. Column of Antoninus
8. Mausoleum of Augustus
9. Piazza Navona
10. Ponte Sant' Angelo
11. Bridge of Antoninus
12. Sta. Maria in Trastevere
13. Ponte Fabricio
14. Tiber Island
15. Ponte Sta. Maria (Rotto
16. Valentinian Bridge
17. S. Pietro in Vincoli
18. San Lorenzo fuori le Mura
Ponte Molle
VIA FLAMINIA
VIA SALARIA
VIA NOMENTANA
Tiber
Porta Flaminia
Porta Salaria
Porta Pinciana
Porta Nomentana
Sta. Maria del Popolo
VIA LATA
Castel Sant' Angelo
LEONINE CITY
Nero's Bridge
St. Peter's
Porta Viridaria
Pantheon
VIA PAPALIS
Baths of Diocletian
Sta. Maria Maggiore
Porta Taurina
Porta Septimiana
VIA AURELIA
Porta Aurelia
TRASTEVERE
Sta. Cecilia
Colosseum
Porta Labicana
Sta. Croce
St. John Lateran
Stadium
Porta San Giovanni
Porta Portese
Porta Metronia
VIA TUSCULANA
Baths of Caracalla
Porta Latina
Porta S. Paolo
Porta Appia
VIA LATINA
VIA PORTUENSE
VIA OSTIENSE
VIA APPIA
S. Paolo fuori le Mura

I: ROME c.1150

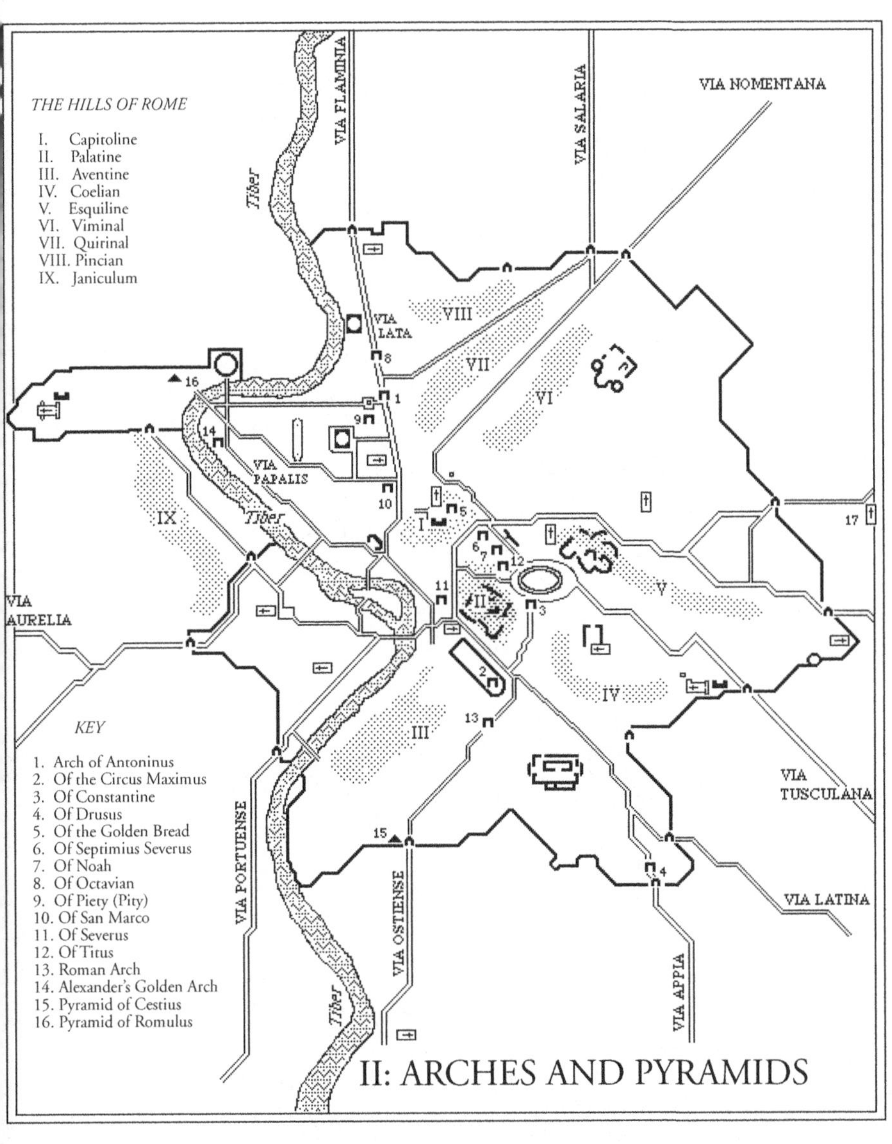
THE HILLS OF ROME
I. Capitoline
II. Palatine
III. Aventine
IV. Coelian
V. Esquiline
VI. Viminal
VII. Quirinal
VIII. Pincian
IX. Janiculum
VIA FLAMINIA
VIA SALARIA
VIA NOMENTANA
Tiber
VIA LATA
VIA PAPALIS
VIA AURELIA
VIA PORTUENSE
VIA OSTIENSE
VIA APPIA
VIA LATINA
VIA TUSCULANA
KEY
1. Arch of Antoninus
2. Of the Circus Maximus
3. Of Constantine
4. Of Drusus
5. Of the Golden Bread
6. Of Septimius Severus
7. Of Noah
8. Of Octavian
9. Of Piety (Pity)
10. Of San Marco
11. Of Severus
12. Of Titus
13. Roman Arch
14. Alexander's Golden Arch
15. Pyramid of Cestius
16. Pyramid of Romulus
II: ARCHES AND PYRAMIDS

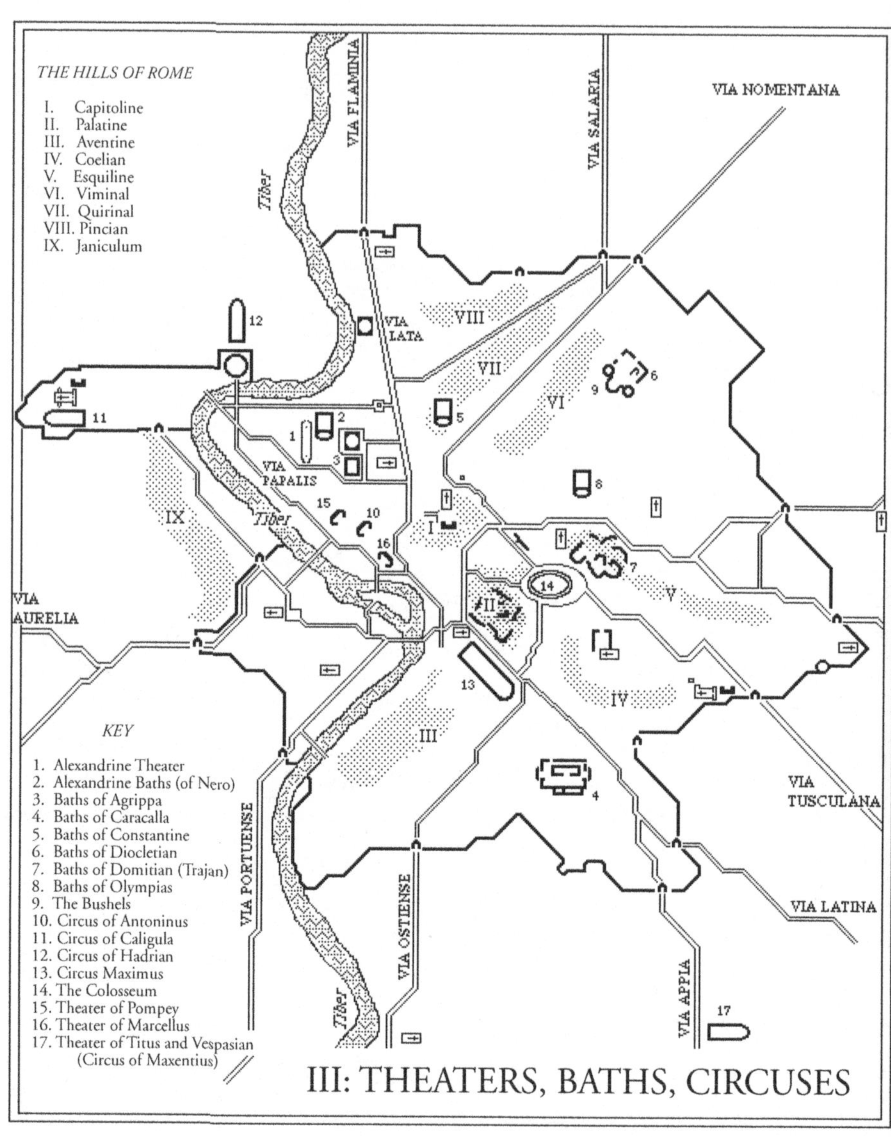

III: THEATERS, BATHS, CIRCUSES

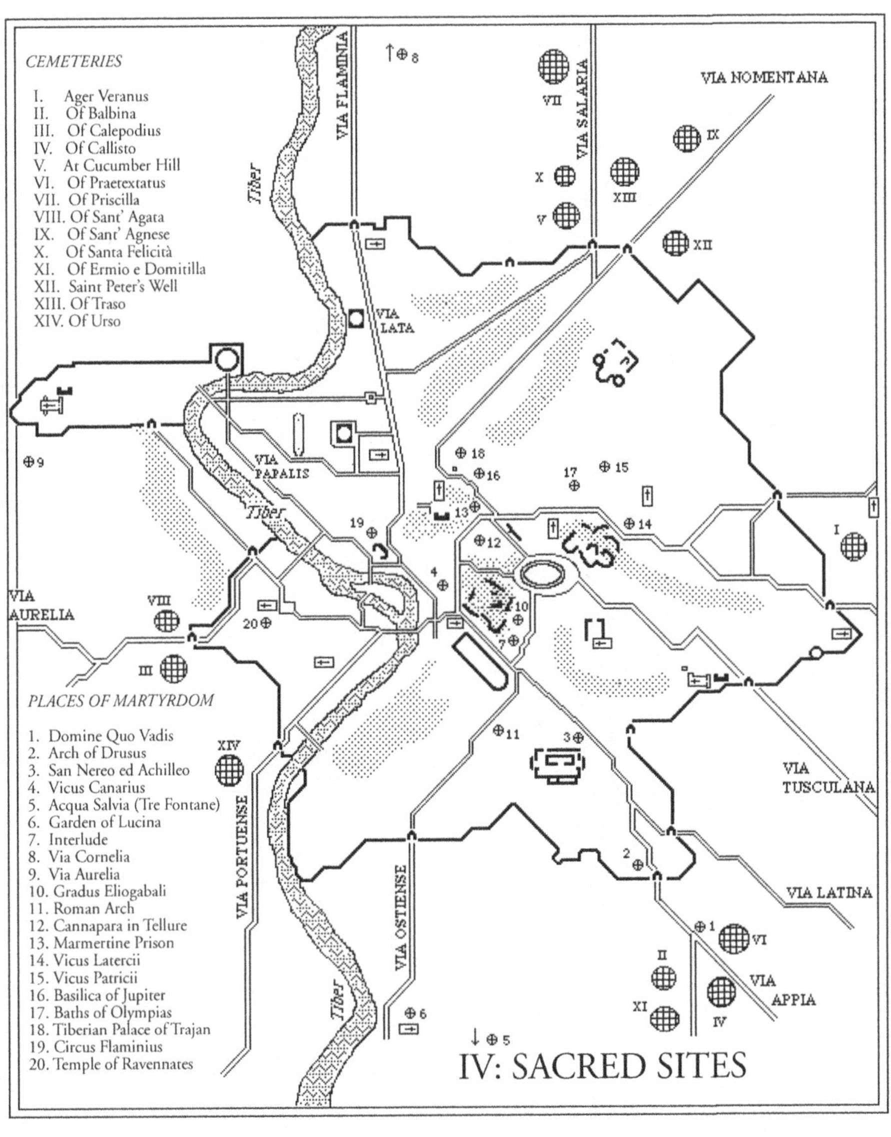
CEMETERIES
I. Ager Veranus
II. Of Balbina
III. Of Calepodius
IV. Of Callisto
V. At Cucumber Hill
VI. Of Praetextatus
VII. Of Priscilla
VIII. Of Sant' Agata
IX. Of Sant' Agnese
X. Of Santa Felicità
XI. Of Ermio e Domitilla
XII. Saint Peter's Well
XIII. Of Traso
XIV. Of Urso
PLACES OF MARTYRDOM
1. Domine Quo Vadis
2. Arch of Drusus
3. San Nereo ed Achilleo
4. Vicus Canarius
5. Acqua Salvia (Tre Fontane)
6. Garden of Lucina
7. Interlude
8. Via Cornelia
9. Via Aurelia
10. Gradus Eliogabali
11. Roman Arch
12. Cannapara in Tellure
13. Marmertine Prison
14. Vicus Latercii
15. Vicus Patricii
16. Basilica of Jupiter
17. Baths of Olympias
18. Tiberian Palace of Trajan
19. Circus Flaminius
20. Temple of Ravennates
VIA FLAMINIA
VIA SALARIA
VIA NOMENTANA
VIA LATA
VIA PAPALIS
Tiber
VIA AURELIA
VIA PORTUENSE
VIA OSTIENSE
VIA TUSCULANA
VIA LATINA
VIA APPIA
IV: SACRED SITES

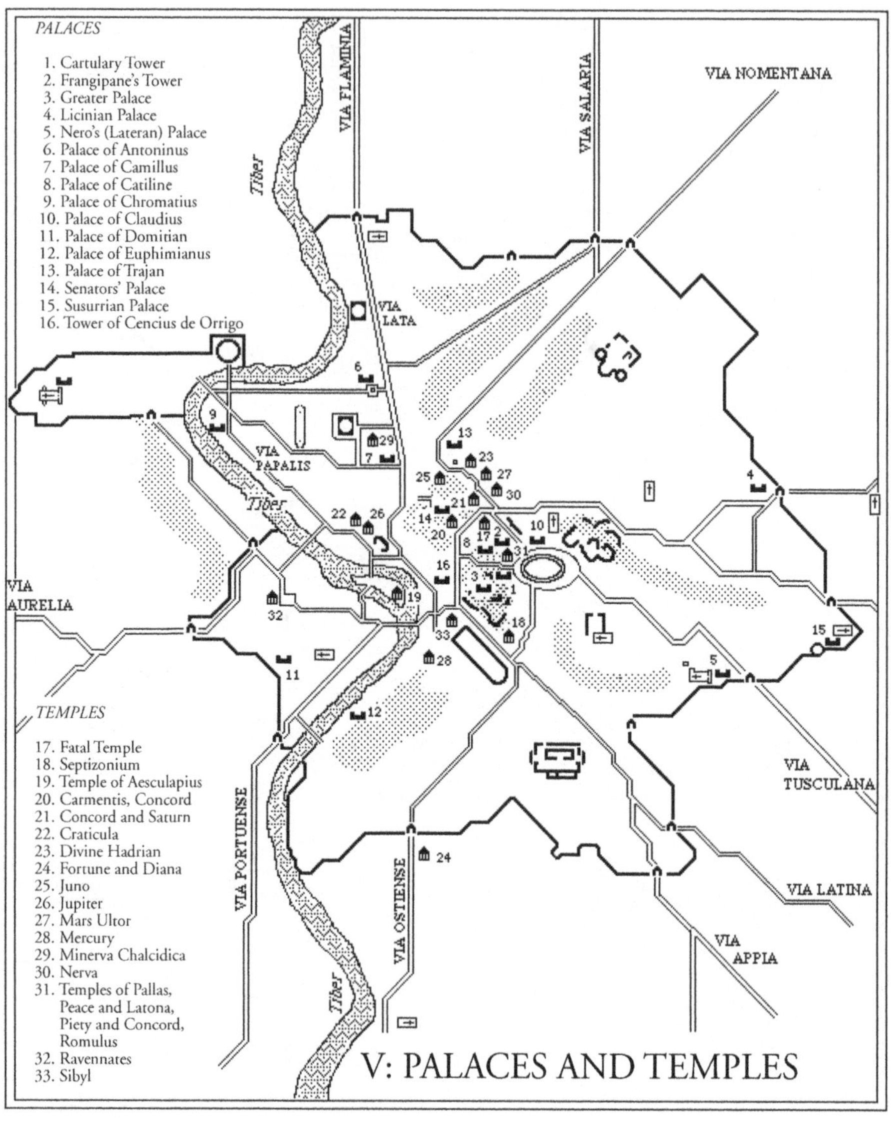

V: PALACES AND TEMPLES

BIBLIOGRAPHY

Adinolfi, Pasquale, *Roma nell'età di mezzo,* Rome, 1881-82.

Amadi, E. *Roma turrita,* Rome, 1943.

Armellini, Mariano, *Gli antichi cimiteri cristiani di Roma e d'Italia,* Rome, 1893.

———. *Le chiese di Roma dal secolo* IV *al XIX,* rev. ed. by C. Cecchelli. Rome, 1942.

Baronio, Cecare, *Martyrologium romanum,* Venice: Marcum Antonium Zalterium, 1597.

Barraclough, Geoffrey, *The Medieval Papacy,* New York, 1979.

Barraconi, Giuseppe, *Rioni di Roma,* Rome 1974.

Becker, Wilhelm Adolf, *Handbuch der römischen Alterthümer nach den Quellen bearbeit,* Leipzig: Weidmann, 1843–67.

Blue Guide to Rome and Environs, London: Ernest Benn Ltd., 1975.

Bolland, John, *Acta sanctorum,* ed. Geoffrey Henschenius, S. J., Antwerp: Ioannem Meursium, 1634–1932.

Brentano, Robert, *Rome before Avignon,* New York: Basic Books, 1974.

Broke, Christopher, *The Twelfth Century Renaissance,* New York, 1976.

Bunsen, Christian Karl Josias, *Die Basiliken des Christlichen Roms,* Munich, Knapp, 1843.

Carrettoni, A. M. Collini, L. Cozza and G. Gatti, *La pianta marmorea di Roma antica,* Rome, 1960.

Castagnoli, Ferdinando, C. Cecchelli, G. Giovannoni, and M. Zocca, *Topografia e urbanistica di Roma,* Bologna, Istituto di Studi Romani, 1958.

Cecchelli, *Monumenti cristiano-eretici di Roma,* Rome, 1944.

Chenu, M. D., O. P., *Nature, Man, and Society in the Twelfth Century,* edited by Jerome Taylor and Lester K. Little, Chicago, 1979.

Clarac, Charles Othon, F. J. B., *Musée de Sculpture Antique et Moderne,* Paris: Imprimerie Royale, 1841–53.

Comparetti, Domenico P. A., *Virgilio nel Medio Evo,* Livorno: 1872.

———. *Vergil in the Middle Ages,* trans. by E. F. M. Benecke, intro. by Robinson Ellis, New York: G. E. Stechert & Co., 1929.

de Rossi, Jean Baptist, *Piante icnografiche e prospettiche di Roma anteriori al secola XVI,* Rome, 1879.
———. *Roma sotterranea cristiana,* Rome, 1864.
———. *Bullettino. di archaeologia. cristiana,* 1867.
———. *Bullettino. dell'Istituto archeologico germanico,* 1884.
D'Onofrio, C. *Le fontane di Roma,* Rome, 1957.
———. *Gli obelischi di Roma,* Rome, 1968.
Duchesne, L., "L'auteur des Mirabilia," *Mélanges d'Archéologie et d'Histoire de l'Ecole Française de Rome* 24 (1904): 479ff.
Eckhart, Johann Georg von, *Corpus historicum medii aevi,* Leipzig, 1723.
Effemeridi litterarie di Roma, Rome, 1820– .
Enikel, Jansen, *Weltbuch,* in *Monumenta Germanica Historica* 3, Hanover, 1891–1900.
Fauno, Lucio, *Compendio di Roma antica,* Venice: Michele Tramezzino, 1522, in *Delle Antichità della Città di Roma,* Venice, 1553.
Ferrari, G., *Early Roman Monasteries,* Vatican City, 1957.
Fontana, Domenico, *Della trasportatione obelisco vaticano,* Rome: D. Basa, 1590.
Frutaz, Amato Pietro, ed., *Le piante di Roma,* Rome, 1962.
Gardthausen, Viktor Emil, *Rerum gestarum libri qui supersunt,* reprint of 1874 edition, Stuttgart, 1967.
Gibbon, Edward, *The History of the Decline and Fall of the Roman Empire,* 3 vols., New York, 1920–35.
Giustiniani, Vincenzo, *Galleria Giustiniani del Marchese Vincenzo Giustiniani,* Rome, 1631– .
Gnoli, U., *Topografia e toponomastica di Roma medioevale e moderna,* Rome, 1939.
Graf, Arturo, *Roma nella memoria e nelle immaginazioni del Medio Evo,* 2 vols., Torino, 1915.
Grasse, Johann Georg Theodor, *Beitrage zur Litteratur und Sage des Mittelalters,* Dresden, 1850.
Gregorovius, Ferdinand A., *History of the City of Rome in the Middle Ages,* transl. Annie Hamilton, 8 vols. in 13, London, 1894–1900; reprint New York, 2000–2004.
Haskins, Charles Homer, *The Renaisssance of the Twelfth Century,* Cleveland and New York, 1966.
Hibbert, Christopher, *Rome: The Biography of a City,* New York, 1985.
Hülsen, C., *Le chiese di Roma nel Medio Evo,* Florence, 1927.
Jordan, Henry, *Topographie der Stadt Rom im Alterthum,* 2 vols., Berlin, 1871.
Krautheimer, Richard, et al., *Corpus basilicarum christianarum Romae,* 4 vols., Vatican City, 1937–77.
———. *Rome. Profile of a City, 312–1308,* Princeton, 1980.

Ladner, G., *Die Papstbildnisse des Altertums und des Mittelalters,* 2 vols., Vatican City, 1941 and 1970.
Lanciani, Rodolfo. *Atti della Pontificia accademia romana dei Nuovi Lincei.*
———. *Forma urbis Romae,* Milan, 1896.
———. *The Destruction of Ancient Rome,* New York, 1899.
———. *Storia degli Scavi di Roma,* 4 vols., Rome, 1902–12.
Lugli, G., *I monumenti antichi di Roma e suburbio,* Rome, 1930–40.
Mabillon, Jean, Museum Italicum, 2 vols. Paris: Montalent, 1724.
Mallius, Petrus, *History of the Basilica of Saint Peter,* in *Acta sanctorum,* vol. 27, June 7, appendix 51, Paris and Rome, 1867.
Martinelli, Fioravante, *Roma ex ethnica sacra,* Rome, 1653.
Matthew, Donald, *Atlas of Medieval Europe,* New York, 1983.
Masson, Georgina, *Companion Guide to Rome,* Englewood Cliffs, 1983.
Mittarelli, J.B., *Annales Camaldulenses,* Venice, 1758.
Muratori, Ludovico Antonio, *Rerum italicarum scriptores,* Bologna, 1938.
Nibby, *Roma nel MDCCCXXXVIII,* Rome, 1839.
Nichols, Francis Morgan, ed. and transl., *Mirabilia urbis Romae,* London, Ellis & Elvey, 1889.
———. *The Roman Forum,* London: Longmans, 1877.
Ozanam, Frédéric, *Documents inédits pour servir à l'histoire litéraire de l'Italia,* Paris, 1850.
Papencordt, Felix, *Geschichte der Stadt Rom im Mittelalter,* ed. Constantin Höfler, Paderborn, 1857.
Partner, Peter, *The Lands of Saint Peter,* London, 1972.
Pietrangleli, C., ed., *Guide rionali di Roma,* 1967.
Poggio Bracciolini, *Opera omnia,* ed. Riccardo Fubini, 4 vols., Turin, 1964–69.
Romano, P., *Roma nella sue strade e nelle sue piazze,* Rome, 1950.
Schudt, L., *Le guide di Roma,* Vienna and Augsburg, 1930.
Urlichs, Carl Ludwig, *Codex topographicus urbis Romae,* Wurzburg, 1871.
Valentini, R., and G. Zucchetti, *Codice topografico della città di Roma,* 4 vols, Rome, 1940–53.
Walley, Daniel, *The Italian City-Republics,* New York, 1978.
William of Malmesbury, *Chronicle of the Kings of England,* ed. and transl. J. A. Giles, London, 1847.
Wright, John Kirtland, *Geographical Lore of the Time of the Crusades,* New York, 1925; reprint New York, 1965.

INDEX

This Book Was Completed on August 23, 1986
At Italica Press, New York, New York.
It Was Set in Garamond and It is
Printed on 60-lb, Acid-Free,
Natural Paper by
BookSurge,
U. S. A./
E. U.
❖

Made in the USA
Monee, IL
04 February 2023

26360661R00100